THE
Country
GARDEN

Country Homes & Gardens®
New York

Copyright © Eaglemoss Publications Ltd 1999
Based on *The Country Look*

First published in North America in 2000 by
Country Homes & Gardens
1271 Avenue of the Americas
New York, NY 10020

Library of Congress Cataloging-in-Publication Data available

ISBN 0-965-005703

Printed in the United States of America

10 9 8 7 6 5 4 3 2 1

CONTENTS

INTRODUCTION

The words "country garden" can evoke many different images—artfully haphazard drifts of wildflowers swaying in the sunlight; a secluded corner of cultivated woodland, carpeted with bluebells and foliage plants; or the glorious profusion of floral colors, shapes, and scents enveloping an English cottage.

However different these images may be, in all of them the plants themselves are the main attraction, and the goal is to allow them—within reason—to flourish as naturally as possible. A country garden is the antithesis of the formal garden, with everything planted in straight lines, or the minimalist garden, in which a few plants are displayed virtually as *objets d'art* against paving and architecture. The country garden celebrates nature.

Happily, you can enjoy country gardening even if you don't live in the country. Even a tiny patio in town, a roof garden, or a window box can be given a country flavor through a wise choice of plants and the right kind of care and attention.

In the following pages you'll find suggestions for selecting and growing different kinds of plants, such as climbers, bulbs, and small trees; ideas for growing plants in containers and indoors and for displaying them in cut flower arrangements; and detailed portraits of some favorite country garden plants, including, among others, poppies, campanulas, climbing roses, and clematis. Ideas for combining different plants for visual contrast or harmony are also provided.

We hope that these ideas will inspire you to bring a little of the country into your own garden.

1
What Makes a Country Garden?

COUNTRY CLIMBERS

Wherever you live, you can transform your garden into a leafy rural retreat by filling it with climbers.

House and garden walls and fences can become solid backdrops of flowers and foliage, with dull-colored, clashing or damaged surfaces cleverly concealed at the same time.

In small and city gardens, climbers are an ideal way of tipping the balance between hard surfaces and plants and introducing a welcome, large-scale seasonal element.

Even if you have no open ground, you can grow many climbers very successfully in a variety of large containers, creating a genuine country look.

Free-standing vertical features, such as arches, pergolas, or trees, can take on a new dimension draped in romantic, old-fashioned flowers and foliage, and even horizontal surfaces, such as banks or the area under trees, can be covered with climbers when they are used as ground cover.

Roses and clematis are considered

▲ **Old-fashioned favorite**
A wisteria-covered rustic arch frames a stone pedestal and urn, creating a semi-wild, romantic focal point.

traditional standby plants, and these are covered in detail elsewhere but there are many other attractive and easy-to-grow climbers from which to choose. These plants offer an enormous variety of colorful flowers, foliage, fragrance, and ornamental fruit.

▲ High-key contrast
The fiery red autumn foliage of this attractive Boston ivy enhances the orange berries of the evergreen firethorn.

▼ Instant cover
*The huge and rampant silver lace vine (*Fallopia baldschuanica*) is ideal for concealing eyesores, such as old toolsheds or gutters.*

Types of climbers

In nature, climbers use other plants as support for their own, weak young stems. A few, such as ivy, Boston ivy, and climbing hydrangea, are self-clinging, using modified tendrils or aerial roots.

Once established against walls or up trees, self-clinging climbers need no additional support but make maintenance difficult and can damage walls.

Others, like honeysuckle, climb by twining stems or leaf tendrils around a support, or, in the case of climbing roses, by clinging with their thorns. They need trellis, wires, strong netting, poles, or other plants to clamber over.

Some popular "climbers," such as *Chaenomeles* and *Pyracantha*, are actually strong stemmed and self-supporting but can be trained to grow tight against a wall. Besides woody climbers, there are herbaceous climbers.

Buying and caring for climbers

Buy in fall or spring for the best choice. Many garden centers group climbers separately.

Plant whenever the soil isn't frozen or waterlogged. Dig the soil, remove weeds, and add well-rotted organic matter. Make the hole at least lft (30cm) from a wall, since soil next to a wall is bone-dry. Remove the plant from its pot and place in the hole, angled toward the support and with the top of the rootball roughly level with the soil. Backfill, firming as you go, water well, and sprinkle with bonemeal.

Care: Water in dry weather and provide supports. Feed and mulch annually, and tie in, prune, and protect from pests, diseases, and frost.

▶ Autumn glory
The brilliant red foliage of the ornamental vine (Amelopsis aconitifolia) contrasts with the foamy white flowers of the evergreen, self-climber Pileostegia viburnoides, or tanglehead.

▼ Passion flowers and fruit
Passiflora caerulea *thrives against a sunny wall, producing its exquisite flowers followed in the summer by attractive, edible fruit.*

Choosing climbers

As with most garden plants, flowers are often the initial attraction, but foliage is equally important, and there are practical considerations, too.

Flowers should fit the color scheme and ideally have a long display season. Some are scented, others flower early or late when color is welcome, and a few, such as wisteria, take years to flower.

Foliage can be evergreen, providing year-round cover, or deciduous, often with spring or fall tints. It can be plain green, variegated, or different-colored; large or small, lacy or sculptural.

Ornamental fruit is an autumnal feature, but may last well into winter, attract birds, or be edible, as with passion flower or flowering quince. With a few species, you need female plants.

Size should match available space, although pruning can control size. Some climbers, such as most honeysuckles, are quick-growing; others are much slower.

Growing conditions should match a climber's needs, otherwise its health and looks suffer. Some climbers, such as ivy, grow almost anywhere, while others, such as wisteria, need sun to flower well, and a few, such as winter jasmine and blue passion flower, are semi-hardy. Some, such as clematis, like alkaline soil; others hate it.

tip

Making climbers cling
Guide newly planted self-clinging climbers toward the wall with an angled pole, and gently affix the shoots to the wall with waterproof adhesive tape. Remove them once the shoots are clinging.

Decorative ideas with climbers

Combine two or three different climbers with harmonizing flowers for display seasons that follow on, one after another, to create a rich effect.

A combination of firethorn, ivy, and winter jasmine is one possibility; wisteria, honeysuckle, and ornamental grape vine, such as *Vitis vinifera* "Brandt," another. If you include an evergreen climber, it will see you through the winter.

Use old fruit trees as supports for moderately vigorous climbers; try wisteria or honeysuckle as a change from clematis and roses.

Grow tender climbers, such as Chinese jasmine (*Trachelospermum jasminoides*), in pots for displaying outdoors in late spring and summer and indoors the rest of the year. When you move them out, plant lobelia, sweet alyssum, petunias, or other colorful annuals around the edge.

For unusual large-scale ground cover, let climbing hydrangea, yellow-veined honeysuckle (*Lonicera japonica* "Aureo-reticulata"), or rambling roses scramble over the ground. Make sure there are no shrubs nearby, or the climbers may attempt to climb.

For a waterfall effect let climbers such as ornamental vines hang over high retaining walls.

Herbaceous climbers such as glory flower (*Eccremocarpus scaber*), which is perennial in zones 9 and 10, and the annual climbing nasturtium (*Tropaeolum majus*), look lovely scrambling over

shrubs, such as Mexican orange, whose display season is over or softening the formality of a clipped hedge.

For maximum fragrance grow scented climbers, such as honeysuckle and summer jasmine, around doors or windows or next to a patio or sitting-out area. A bower of fragrant climbers over a garden bench makes a wonderfully old-fashioned focal point for any cottage-style garden.

▲ *Flowers and fragrance*
Honeysuckle (Lonicera periclymenum " Belgica") and Japanese wisteria (Wisteria floribunda) combine to provide an early summer show.

▼ *Candy pink and white*
Actinidia kolomikta, *a slender, twining climber with boldly variegated foliage, enlivens a sunny, sheltered wall.*

◄ *A touch of sun*
Yellow centered, the golden hop (Humulus lupulus " Aureus") is a herbaceous perennial twining climber widely grown in England, that dies back to ground level in the fall and sprouts again each spring.

ROMANTIC CLIMBING ROSES

Summer wouldn't be the same without climbing roses, transforming walls, arches, fences, and pergolas into sheets of color and filling the garden with fragrance. Some climbing roses flower profusely for a week or two in late spring or early summer; some others flower repeatedly, carrying a second, smaller show of blooms in the fall; and many others are perpetual-flowering, blooming all summer and well into fall.

Climbing roses have hooked thorns, by which they attach themselves to and scramble over shrubs and trees in the wild. In the garden, they are usually trained into a permanent framework of rigid, woody stems with flowering side shoots, or laterals. They range from 6 to 30ft (1.8–9m) or more high.

The flowers, carried singly or in clusters, are mostly double but can be semi-double or single. Climbing roses can be white, pink, yellow, apricot, orange, red, crimson, bicolored, or multicolored. Their old-fashioned charm is ideal for cottage gardens, but they will fit easily into any garden style.

Choosing climbing roses

The flower color should fit into your general garden scheme and, if you want roses for cutting, your interior decor. In addition to the color, the scent and shape of the flowers should appeal to you, but try to match the plant's vigor and eventual size to available space. Depending on the size of your garden, you may prefer either a brief but stunning floral display or a more modest but longer-lasting one.

Some climbing rose varieties are naturally hardy and resist pests and diseases, while a few are tender or prone to mildew and other problems. If in doubt, check with garden center staff, or look in a rose catalog.

▶ **A flush of pink**
Climbing roses look wonderful grown against a wall at the back of a bed of perennials, especially if you choose a type that will flower all through the summer, like "Bantry Bay." This is a vigorous floribunda-type climber which tends to straggle unless it is regularly pruned. It has vivid pink semi-double flowers which are borne on open trusses (flowering sprays) intermittently throughout the summer months.

Decorative ideas

Dramatic contrasts White and pale roses are especially effective in the evening and against a dark backdrop. (White roses, like many other white flowers, tend to be scented, to attract night-flying pollinators.) Dark roses look best against a pale background like a white wall or light green foliage. Dark colors also have extra impact when seen close up, beside a patio or by a living-room window.

For quick contrast, grow annual blue-flowered morning glories through a climbing rose. For permanent summer contrast, interplant climbing roses and deep-violet wishbone flowers (*Torenia fournierii*). For more subtle contrast in both form and texture, try growing yellow-flowered honeysuckles and yellow roses together, or pink-flowered honeysuckles with pink roses.

Suiting the setting Single-flowered varieties look less formal than double-flowered ones and are ideal for country-style gardens. A climbing rose takes its cue from its setting. The same variety can look informal trained over a frame ranch-style house, or formal against the façade of a mansion.

Plant partners Most plants combine well with climbing roses, but some, such as harmonizing or contrasting clematis, are traditional partners.

Scent supplements To provide fragrance near unscented climbing roses, grow regal lilies, lavender, or flowering tobacco plants nearby.

Special places Compact climbing roses are ideal for training up pillars. Use sturdy, 10ft (3m) high wooden posts, or a conifer trunk, sunk 2ft (60cm) in the ground. Plant a rose at its base, or a pair or trio of pale, medium, and dark-toned roses. Train the main stems spirally up the post—the nearer the horizontal the woody stems, the more prolific the flowering. To add height to a formal or informal rose garden, grow climbing roses spirally up poles set among rose bushes. On a hot, sunny wall, grow a passion flower or the delicate, silvery leaved *Senecio leucostachys* through a pink or scarlet-flowered rose.

On a north-facing wall, grow the silvery-pink "New Dawn" with hostas, ferns, and pink and white impatiens at its feet. On an arbor, train wisteria to hang down from the roof, and climbing roses up the supports. The unusual miniature climbing rose "Nozomi" grows 5ft (1.5m) high, if trained, but if left to spread it makes excellent ground cover, with trusses of single pink flowers. *Rosa filipes* "Kiftsgate" can spread 50ft (15m). With its huge trusses of sweetly scented, creamy-white flowers, it is ideal for screening an ugly shed or growing up a large tree; or use the slightly smaller, semi-evergreen "Mermaid" with sulfur-yellow flowers which grows to 30ft (9m).

Popular climbing rose types

In many garden centers tall-growing roses are grouped together as "climbers," but even within such a category there are different types of roses. Here we are

---

Caring for climbing roses

Most climbing roses are sold bare-rooted in clear packs or in containers.

Buy young, vigorous plants with plump wood, well-balanced growth, and, since most are grafted, a strong join between the rooted stock and named variety, or scion. If plants are bare-rooted, avoid any with signs of premature growth; if in full growth, the leaves should look healthy, with no sign of black spot or other problems.

Site Choose a sunny site, though some varieties flourish in light shade. Deep, rich, moist but well-drained soil is best, with added garden or sterilized organic compost. Use loam-based compost for containers.

Plant bare-rooted roses when dormant, others at any time of year provided the ground isn't frozen or waterlogged, at least 12in (30cm) from a wall.

Care: Water well in dry weather, feed regularly, and mulch in spring. Tie to trellis, wires, or other support, and tie in shoots regularly. Deadhead to encourage further flowering. From the second year onward, prune side shoots back to two or three buds from the stem in fall or winter, and cut out any old, weak, or damaged wood.

dealing with large-flowered climbers with their rigid, thick canes, as opposed to rambling roses, which have thinner, suppler stems, clusters of smaller flowers and a tendency to scramble rather than ascend. Since all young roses may look the same when you are buying them, knowing the type helps you to choose wisely and to care for them well.

Climbing sports are climbing versions of hybrid tea and floribunda roses, such as the white-flowered "Climbing Iceberg." They tend to be more attractive than the shrub versions, carrying their flowers in a more natural-looking way. Some are only moderately hardy and flower only once a summer.

Modern climbing roses, such as "New Dawn" and "Compassion," are hardy and long flowering—many with hybrid tea-like blooms. Most grow to less than 10ft (3m), and are perfect for training around pillars.

◄ **Vertical gardening**
The buttercup-yellow "Climbing Allgold," a climbing version of the floribunda "Allgold," provides high-level interest on this English cottage wall, with the blue-purple flowers of the clematis "Lasurstern" lower down. At ground level, mounds of valerian complete a trio of bright country colors.

Noisettes are old-fashioned, repeat-flowering climbers, needing a warm wall in a warm climate (from zone 8 south) to thrive. The pink-tinged yellow "Gloire de Dijon," also known as "Old Glory Rose," is one favorite—early, perpetual, and hardier than other noisettes.

Shrub roses as climbers Some English shrub roses, such as the apricot-pink-flowered "Abraham Darby," can be trained as climbers, as can some vigorous modern shrub roses, such as the golden-yellow "Goldbusch."

▲ **Dawn pink**
The ever popular climber "New Dawn" has fragrant pearl-pink flowers. Here the rose is rampaging up a wall; it can easily climb to 20ft (6m), but it can also be pruned hard and trained as a pillar rose.

▼ **Fruit and flowers**
An old fruit tree makes an ideal support for this silvery-pink rose. Plant on the sunny side of the trunk, and tie in the shoots until they find their way into the branches.

▲ Black and white background
Black-painted trellis against a white wall makes a modern, almost oriental, setting for the brilliant orange-red, semi-double blooms of floribunda rose "Sarabande." This vivid rose has been trained to climb, but it is usually seen in its shrubby form.

tip

Cut roses
To help cut stems take up water, re-cut them at an angle, and make a vertical, upward slit ½in (12mm) deep. Plunge the flowers almost up to their necks in water and leave for several hours, ideally overnight, before arranging.

▲ Roses all the way
Create a delightful rose walk by training roses over a series of wooden or plastic arches. The roses here are old-fashioned noisettes, climbing tea roses, and pillar roses in whites and various shades of pink.

◄ Up and over
A bold contrast is created by training a red-flowered and a white-flowered climber to meet and mingle on a trellis, as here, or on an arch or pergola. A charming alternative would be to blend pink and white or, for a touch of subtlety, two shades of pink or two of yellow.

GRACEFUL GARDEN ARCHES

As decorative features in their own right, arches and pergolas provide the perfect excuse and support for a vast array of climbing plants. Depending on the style, these arches can add a romantic, old-fashioned country-garden look or a modern touch. They are also useful for visually linking the garden to the house, provided they are built in the same material and similar styles.

In a new or older treeless garden, arches and pergolas are especially valuable for providing instant height, to complement and contrast with the horizontal line of the garden's lawns and low-growing plants. Furthermore, if you plant fairly quick-growing climbers to grow over them, you'll find that the garden will take on an air of maturity that is beyond its years.

Arches can be rounded, pointed, or flat, but they tend to be single-span structures, while pergolas are larger in scale, with several spans, usually extending over paths and sometimes even incorporating seats.

▼ *Making an entrance*
Chinese wisteria frames a brick archway over an unusual moon gate.

Choosing an arch

The factors to consider include personal taste, budget, and available space. Decide whether you want a kit form, pre-assembled, or custom-built structure, and choose a style to suit your particular garden.

Simple arches tend to be neutral in design terms. White-painted arches stand out more than wood ones, but when clothed in climbers all arches look pretty similar.

Brick and stone arches create a strong sense of permanence and should be chosen to repeat the material of nearby walls or other stands.

Softwood arches are popular, and can be pre-assembled. They should be pressure-impregnated with a preservative to retard rotting. Rustic arches look charming, but are more likely to rot.

Hardwood arches and pergolas made from teak are costly, but long lasting.

Galvanized, painted, or plastic-coated steel arches come in reproduction Victorian or modern styles.

Iron frames for arching fruit trees and climbers like wisteria are sturdy and long lasting, but again can be costly.

Situating arches and pergolas

An arch or pergola is an automatic focal point; it can also be used to frame a view, garden statue, or bench. Pergolas can straddle a path, create shade and shelter over a patio, or link a house to its garage or carport. A climber-covered pergola can also be used to hide an ugly view.

Plants for arches

As with any garden plant, choose climbers that suit your garden's soil and color scheme. Consider the season and duration of flowering, and try to match the rate of growth to the size of arch. Check labels and, if necessary, seek advice. If the arch needs painting regularly, avoid plants like wisteria that do not die back in winter.

Many climbers thrive in sun, but a few, such as ivy and wintercreeper enonymous (*E. fortunei*), like shade. Most prefer well-drained but moisture-retentive, weed-free soil.

Woody climbers include species and hybrid clematis, ranging from 6 to 30ft (1.8–9m) in height and flowering from early spring to fall. Common jasmine (*Jasminum officinale*) carries scented white flowers in summer. There are countless climbing and pillar roses; and pink, purple, and white forms of wisteria.

Perennial climbers die back each year; they can grow up to 10–20ft (3–6m) in height and include the perennial beach pea (*Lathyrus japonicus*) with pink flowers, and Serbian bellflower (*Campanula porscharskyana*), which has mauve flowers.

Climbing annuals which must be planted each year include nasturtium, sweet pea, and Japanese hop (*Humulus japonicus*), with attractively notched leaves. In mild, frost-free gardens, ivy-leaf pclargoniums and blue-flowered Cape leadwort can be trained up arches.

Creative ideas

Try fixing hanging baskets to the sides of an arch; these can be filled with lobelias and trailing fuchsias to give the garden extra summer color.

Another idea is to fix an arch against a wall to create a niche. Fill the niche with wall-hung baskets, a statue, or a flower-filled urn to create a rustic look. You can make a secret meeting place in

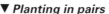

tip

Shade-loving climbers
If you have an archway in a shady corner of your garden, try growing ivy, wintercreeper eunymous (*E. fortunei*), or hydrangea (*H. petiolaris*) for a colorful effect.

▲ **Eye-catching focal point**
*These classic white arches support a variety of climbing plants including golden hops (*Humulus lupulus*), red and pink roses, and honeysuckle.*

▼ **Planting in pairs**
Honeysuckle and clematis complement each other beautifully. Here the contrasting colors liven up one column of a brick and wood pergola.

a similar way by placing a bench underneath a flower-covered arch. To emphasize an arch, you could try placing a pair of stone columns on either side of it.

An inexpensive and simple arch can be made with tall trellis panels fixed to sturdy posts. Provided the height and width for the arch is generous, you could create a pergola by erecting several, identical, kit-form or pre-assembled arches in a straight row.

▶ **Rustic beauty**
A profusion of mixed-colored rambling and climbing roses entwines the rustic softwood arches in this delightful old-fashioned country-cottage garden.

▼ **Fragrant welcome**
Sturdy honeysuckle clambers over a stone arch, softening its hard edges and creating a pleasing entrance to the garden, while it visually links the arch to the wooden fence.

Ornamental and edible

Many garden vegetables, such as peas, string beans, and some squashes, are naturally climbing and can be easily trained up arches. Their hanging crops make a decorative feature in a vegetable patch. Buy tall-growing, not dwarf, varieties, and follow the instructions. Choose rich, well-drained but moisture-retentive soil and a sunny spot.

Beans are naturally twining and self-supporting; small squashes—normally allowed to sprawl—must be tied in as they grow. To keep the soil healthy, avoid growing the same crop in the same place year after year.

Grapes are a popular climbing fruit, and a vine-covered pergola is a joy to sit under. Choose a variety that suits your soil and local climate. Grapes are long-lived plants, but need pruning. Chinese gooseberry, *Actinidia chinensis*, is also a fruiting climber with handsome foliage. To ensure crops, it is necessary to grow male and female plants together.

If space allows, train espaliered apple over a sturdy pergola to create a romantic walkway. Again, pruning is vital. In warm gardens, cucumbers and even melons can be grown over arches.

▼ **Elegant and edible**
Fruiting and blooming scarlet runner beans cover a simply constructed wood and wire mesh arch in an ornamental vegetable garden.

▲ **Traditional choice**
Grapevines, with their decorative, pendent fruits, are ideal for training up arches and make a natural focal point in the garden.

▼ **Split-level display**
Climbing squash festoon this metal pergola, while colorful nasturtiums cluster beneath, almost covering the garden path.

TRELLIS AND TRELLIS PLANTS

Trellis work can be one of the most attractive and versatile features in the garden. It can be formal or informal, enhance a tiny garden or make an impact in a huge one, and create a romantic, country look, whether the setting is suburban, urban, or truly rural.

Trellis ranges from simple, wall-fixed panels to ornamental garden structures of fantastic complexity, sometimes called "treillage." Depending on the material and style, trellis can be inexpensive, informal, and temporary, or costly, impressive, and permanent. Lightweight, inexpensive trellis is sold at home stores and garden centers. More durable and custom-made trellis must be ordered from specialist dealers.

Traditionally used to support climbing plants, trellis can be decorative as well as practical. White-painted trellis adds sharp, crisp detail to a garden and is especially effective in shade and in winter, when plants are dormant. Trellis in large, free-standing panels or fixed above low walls provides instant privacy; its airy structure creates pleasing shadow patterns and prevents a closed-in feeling. Three-dimensional trellis structures, such as pergolas and porches, can provide a garden with its main focal point.

▼ *Gray on gray*
Trellis doesn't always have to be white. Here, bleached, natural wood trellis blends in with the gray stone wall, allowing the silvery pink flowers of the rambling rose "Mme. Alfred Carrière" to dominate. Lobelia, old-fashioned pinks, and hot-pink Cineraria elegans *add ground-level color.*

Types of trellis

Most trellis is square or diamond, expanding or rigid lattice. Elaborate types may include decorative frames, finials, planters, mirrors or seats.

Wooden trellis is traditional. Inexpensive softwood such as pine or larch needs treating with non-toxic preservative or paint, but still lasts no more than five years or so. Rustic trellis, with bark intact, is also short-lived. Hardwood trellis, such as teak, is costly but long lasting and ideal for permanent features. If left natural, it is maintenance free. If painted or stained, it needs regular maintenance.

Wrought iron and **steel** trellis comes in black or white. Wrought iron trellis is lovely, but heavy and costly. It is long-lasting and needs occasional painting. Painted or plastic-coated steel looks similar but is lighter and less expensive, needs regular maintenance, and may rust.

Plastic trellis is normally available in white or green. Ordinary plastic, though inexpensive and lightweight, tends to become brittle with exposure to the sun and with age. An improved kind of plastic, guaranteed to last twenty years, is available and well worth the extra cost.

Ways with trellis

Fix trellis panels to the sides of the house or garage, and grow climbers over them. For added drama, extend the panels, as round or pointed Gothic arches, above the roof.

Use trellis panels to enclose a formal rose garden, and train climbing and rambling roses over it.

Fix trellis to the railings of steps down to the garden, and grow fragrant climbers over it.

Make a strong trellis "roof" over a sunny patio or gazebo, and grow grape vines or fragrant climbers across it.

Divide a long, thin garden crosswise with tall, climber-covered trellis, with a narrow path through. The trellis will make the garden seem wider and create a sense of mystery about what lies beyond.

In a new, treeless garden, use inexpensive trellis for instant height and privacy around a patio, and plant trees. By the time the trellis rots, the trees will be large enough to make an impact.

Use trellis to screen trash can or clothes-drying areas or, in a large garden, children's play equipment.

Build trellis sides and roof over a garden bench to create a romantic bower.

Plants for trellis

Old-fashioned, ideally fragrant, woody climbers, such as roses, clematis, honeysuckles, and jasmines, are traditional trellis plants. Wisteria, passion flower, cup-and-saucer vine (*Cobaea scandens*), climbing nasturtium (*Tropaeolum majus*), morning glory, and annual or perennial sweet peas are also suitable. Foliage options include ivy, ornamental vines, and kolomikta. For a permanent display, wall-trained shrubs, such as winter jasmine, lemon verbena, Chinese flowering quince, *Escallonia*, *Garrya*, and winter sweet are ideal.

For pots suspended from trellis, most containerized plants will do, but those with a trailing habit, such as ivy-leaved pelargoniums, ivy, trailing lobelias, or fuchsias, are attractive.

For seasonal interest combine early- and late-flowering clematis, or clematis and roses, or winter-flowering jasmine and a spring-flowering clematis.

In spring, fill trellis-hung pots with polyanthus, dwarf tulips, or forget-me-nots, and pansies; in fall, dwarf dahlias and pot chrysanthemums; and in winter,

▶ **Trellis as architecture**
Two wooden trellis "door frames" span a narrow brick path in this subtle, all-green, passage garden. The trellis frame provides support for foliage climbers and emphasizes the perspective, with a glimpse of the colorful garden beyond.

ivy, winter-flowering heathers, or dwarf evergreen eunymous.

Matching plants and trellis Try to match the eventual size, strength, and lifespan of the plant to the size, strength, and lifespan of the trellis. Roses and clematis range from 5ft (1.5m) high to 30ft (9m) or more, so choose with care! Jasmine and honeysuckle are strong growers, but can be cut back hard. Try, too, to match the plant to the aspect, exposure, and soil. If the plant is to be containerized, choose potting mixture to match its needs. Plants with a permanent woody framework, such as wisteria, are unsuitable for trellis that needs maintenance or replacement. Choose instead climbers that are cut back hard each spring, such as some clematis, or herbaceous perennial climbers, such as hops (*Humulus lupulus*), that die back naturally every fall and reappear in spring.

Feed, water, mulch, and prune trellis plants according to type. Remember, though, that soil next to walls tends to be dry and that potting mixture in containers also dries out quickly.

◄ **Increased privacy**
Fixing trellis to the wall can increase the height without creating a solid, walled-in feeling. Here the airy structure hides the ugly wall beyond.

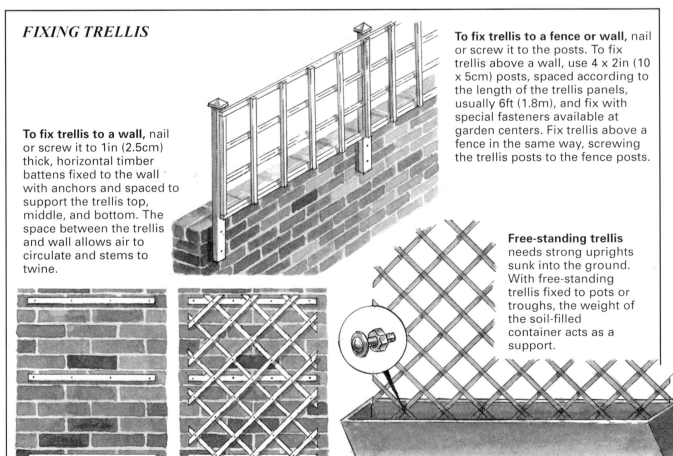

FIXING TRELLIS

To fix trellis to a wall, nail or screw it to 1in (2.5cm) thick, horizontal timber battens fixed to the wall with anchors and spaced to support the trellis top, middle, and bottom. The space between the trellis and wall allows air to circulate and stems to twine.

To fix trellis to a fence or wall, nail or screw it to the posts. To fix trellis above a wall, use 4 x 2in (10 x 5cm) posts, spaced according to the length of the trellis panels, usually 6ft (1.8m), and fix with special fasteners available at garden centers. Fix trellis above a fence in the same way, screwing the trellis posts to the fence posts.

Free-standing trellis needs strong uprights sunk into the ground. With free-standing trellis fixed to pots or troughs, the weight of the soil-filled container acts as a support.

▶ Sweetly scented
Clematis flammula *forms a dense wall of tangled stems bearing fragrant, small, white flowers from late summer to mid-autumn, followed by silky seed heads. This strong-growing species is ideal for training up a large trellis panel over a garage, or up a free-standing trellis to hide an unsightly view.*

▼ Old-fashioned charm
A white-painted wire trellis arch adds an extra dimension to this Victorian façade. Its delicate tracery draws attention to the front door and supports climbing roses—especially appropriate in view of the house's name!

▲ Potted color
For a charming finishing touch, hang small, flower-filled pots from trellis. Here, scarlet and pale pink zonal and ivy-leaved Pelargoniums *fill ceramic pots in wire holders, and enliven a dull brick wall. Impatiens and ivy fill a ground-level pot, continuing the summery theme.*

SPRING FLOWER BORDERS

With a little careful planning a perennial border can be every bit as colorful in spring as in the height of summer.

Besides the ever-popular bulbs such as tulips, daffodils, and hyacinths, there are numerous spring-flowering hardy herbaceous perennials that can be grown in borders and will be at their best at this time. And unlike spring-flowering bulbs, which may need lifting, drying off, storing over summer, and then replanting in the fall, spring-flowering herbaceous perennials can stay put year after year, forming substantial clumps of foliage and flowers.

Spring-flowering perennials range from primroses, a few inches tall, to Solomon's seal, 4ft (1.2m) in height. The time when a given spring flower blooms varies enormously throughout the country; for a succession of blooms, inquire at a garden center to find out when different flowers will bloom in your zone. The flowers can be almost any color, from the clear yellow of *Doronicum orientale* to the warm mauves and pinks of Pasque flower. The

▲ Late-spring splendor
Yellow and orange columbines and rich, maroon-brown flag iris (Iris germanica varieties) create an unusual late-spring show.

leaves vary in size and color; those with dense foliage are useful as ground cover.

By choosing carefully, you can create a display from frosty early spring straight through to the full glory of summer. You can even create a spring country-garden effect on patios or balconies by simply planting pretty spring perennials.

Choosing spring perennials

Besides flower and foliage color, you should consider reliability and length of flowering. Consider, too, height, spread, and growth rate in relation to nearby plants and space available. Tall forms may need staking. For year-round ground cover, choose types with evergreen foliage. Soil, moisture, shelter, and light are also important considerations. Try to harmonize the colors of spring-flowering plants with the foliage of existing shrubs and trees in the garden.

Ideas for spring borders

Spring borders or even clumps of spring-flowering perennials always look pretty when seen from the house. Try planting them next to a path or around the base of a tree. Spring-flowering plants benefit from shelter, and a border at the base of a wall-trained clematis or poet's jasmine in flower would be stunning. Shrubs also provide shelter, and under-planting with perennials gives a "lift" to woody plants such as hydrangeas.

Formal or informal Spring perennials can look formal or informal, according to use. In carefully manicured flower beds they tend to appear formal; in random clumps in a wild garden, the same plants look informal, especially if allowed to self-seed.

Grouping spring perennials Clumps of three or five of one variety make more impact than single plants dotted about, although self-seeded perennials such as hellebores look charming in odd spaces. Grouping white-variegated lungwort is effective in a shady spot.

Plant partners Underplant spring-flowering magnolias such as the star magnolia *(M. stellata)* with a dense swathe of bergenias. This will give a two-level floral display. Combine primroses, lungworts, and Solomon's

▲ **Close harmony**
Pasque flowers and grape hyacinths, with their soft purple and rich blue blooms, make a handsome pair for a sunny spot in mid spring.

seal for a blue, yellow, and white scheme, and include a few lilies-of-the-valley for fragrance. Combine blue Siberian iris, pale pink peonies, and pink and white dicentras for an old-fashioned scheme. The unfurling spring

leaves of hostas make pretty partners for spring-flowering perennials and add interest when the spring display is finished. For poolside interest, plant globeflowers *(Trollius)* and drumstick or candelabrum primulas. Grouping clumps of contrasting foliage—for example, glossy round green leaves of bergenia with the spidery gray-green leaves of *Helleborus foetidus*—is always a very effective planting scheme.

Last-minute fill
If a bare space appears in a spring border, fill it with forget-me-nots or polyanthus, bought in bud.

◄ **Improved form**
"Britten," with its large, apple-blossom pink blooms, is one of the many fine named varieties of bergenia.

▶ **Oriental elegance**
Tiered blooms of Japanese primrose (Primula japonica) repeat the pink and carmine tones of spring-flowering Japanese azaleas.

Popular spring perennials

Barrenwort (*Epimedium* spp. and var. [species and varieties]), evergreen or semi-evergreen, has heart-shaped leaves, and dainty, pink, yellow, or multicolored flowers in early spring. It's a slow-growing plant but eventually gives good ground cover. Plant in rich, moist soil in a sunny or lightly shaded site.

Bergenia (*Bergenia* spp. and var.) has leathery, semi-evergreen leaves and spikes of white or pink flowers in early spring. Plant in sun.

Bleeding heart (*Dicentra* spp. and var.) has ferny leaves and locket-like, hanging flowers in pink and white which appear in late spring.

Columbine (*Aquilegia* spp. and var.) has ferny leaves and nodding spurred flowers, in late spring to early summer, in a range of single and bicolors. The plant self-seeds.

Globeflower (*Trollius* spp. and var.) has lobed leaves and buttercup-like flowers which appear in late spring or summer.

Great leopard's bane (*Doronicum cordatum*) has heart-shaped leaves and yellow daisy-like flowers. It is one of the earliest spring flowers. Plant in moist soil.

Cranesbill (*Geranium* spp. and var.) has deeply cut leaves and saucer-shaped flowers which appear in very late spring, pink in *G. endressii*, magenta in *G. macrohrrhizum*.

Hellebore (*Helleborus* spp. and var.) has lance-shaped leaves and saucer-shaped flowers—green in *H. foetidus* and *H. lividus corsicus*, creamy white to purple in *H. orientalis*, the Lenten rose. It blooms in early spring.

Iris (*Iris* spp. and var.) has grass-like leaves and ruffled flowers in late spring. The profusely blooming *Iris sibirica* has

▲ **Spring contrast**
The creamy-white blooms of a Chinese peony (Paeonia lactiflora) cultivar glow against the rich blue flowers of Geranium grandiflorum.

purple-blue flowers; its cultivars include other hues.

Lungwort (*Pulmonaria* spp. and var.) has white spotted, evergreen leaves and tubular, pink, or blue flowers from early spring. It gives excellent ground cover.

Pasque flower (*Pulsatilla vulgaris*) has feathery leaves and purple, pink, red, or white, cup-shaped flowers in spring.

Peony (*Paeonia* spp. and var.) has deeply cut leaves and bowl-shaped, single or double flowers in white, pink, or red which appear in late spring.

Primrose (*Primula* spp. and var.) has rosettes of leaves, leafless stems, and then five-petaled flowers in late spring, carried singly on polyanthus and primrose types, in clusters on candelabra types, in a range of colors.

Solomon's seal (*Polygonatum* spp.) has arching stems, pairs of rounded leaves and hanging, white, and green bells in late spring.

Spotted dead nettle (*Lamium maculatum*) has evergreen, nettle-like leaves—white in "Beacon Silver"—pink or white flowers in late spring.

Spurge (*Euphorbia* spp.) has unbranched stems of leaves—slender and deciduous in *E. cyparissus*, round, leathery, and evergreen in *E. robbiae*—topped by curious, flower-like, greenish bracts.

▼ **Cottage garden charm**
The charming, locket-shaped blooms of Dicentra spectabilis add an old-fashioned touch to a scheme.

Buying and growing spring perennials

Buy container-grown plants, in fall or spring. In spring, growth buds should be visible.

Site in a sheltered, sunny, or lightly shaded spot according to type, and in fertile, well-drained soil. In containers, use nutrient-rich, loam-based potting mixture.

Plant firmly in well-dug, weed-free soil whenever the ground isn't frozen or waterlogged.

Care: Until the plant is established, keep weeded and watered. Lightly fork over the soil and mulch annually in spring. Stake and dead-head as necessary. Cut back deciduous types to just above ground level in late autumn and protect from frost. Lift and divide quick-growing types every 3–5 years.

LATE-FLOWERING BORDERS

With their colorful, large-scale display of old-fashioned flowers, perennial borders are one of the most popular garden features. For generations, their breathtaking beauty has inspired admiration among gardeners and non-gardeners alike, and an established border in full bloom is, for many people, the epitome of gardening skill.

Although traditional borders consist largely of early summer-flowering perennials, such as delphiniums, lupins and peonies, you can, instead, create a border that is at its best in late summer and early fall—a time of the year that could otherwise be disappointing in the garden. By including a few earlier-flowering perennials, bulbs, biennials, and annuals, you can ensure that the border provides long-lasting interest, ideal in smaller gardens.

Perennial borders are archetypal country garden features, but virtually any sunny or lightly shaded, open garden —whether rural, suburban, or urban, large or small—can have a late perennial border with all its color and country garden charm.

▼ *Perfect evergreen setting*
A yew hedge offsets shades of pink Michaelmas daisies (hybrid asters), red dahlias, bright yellow spoon chrysanthemums, bushy artemisia and a majestic pampas grass.

Types of perennial borders

Perennial borders can be front-facing, backed by a wall, fence, or hedge, with short plants in front, graduating to tall at the back. The increasingly popular island, or all-round, beds are set in lawns, with tallest plants in the center, shortest round the edge.

The beds can be rigidly geometric, such as a rectangle or circle; more informal, based on loose, kidney-shaped curves; or a combination—a border against a wall, for example, can have a straight back and curved front. Very tight curves or complex geometric shapes, however, can look fussy and be difficult to maintain.

You should plan for the border to be at least 5ft (1.5m) wide, to create a feeling of abundance and depth; narrow borders tend to look slightly flat.

Late-flowering perennials

Flower color and form are important, especially in relation to adjacent plants. Consider, too, reliability and length of flowering; red-hot poker flowers, for example, are tough and last for weeks, while lilyturf (*Liriope*) tends to be hidden among the foliage and is vulnerable to weather. Some late-flowering perennials, such as phlox, are short-lived unless lifted and divided regularly, while others, such as *Romneya coulteri*, resent any disturbance. Some, such as Michaelmas daisies, are tough and invasive, while others, such as *Lobelia fulgens*, need cosseting, and still others, such as *Hosta tardiflora*, spread very slowly.

Consider cultivation needs, too. Silver-and-gray-leaved plants need sun; taller plants need staking and shelter; and most border plants need well-drained soil. Many perennial border plants are also excellent for drying and for cut-flower displays.

▶ *Mixed pleasures*
*Bright blue sea holly, yellow red-hot poker (*Kniphofia*), and purple-leaved berberis liven up this lovely late-summer border.*

▼ *Multicolor charm*
*Deep blue agapanthus, white daisy-like anthemis, scarlet montbretia (*Crocosmia*), red fuchsias, and bushy mauve clematis help to fill this perennial border with a profusion of bright summer colors.*

Using perennial borders

Formal or **informal** Perennial borders are by their nature formal, being clearly defined and often having geometric features. In general, however, the denser and thicker the growth, the less formal the overall effect. Tight, self-contained groups of plants surrounded by bare soil tend to look formal. The choice of plants also helps to create a feeling of formality or informality.

Siting Perennial borders can be used to separate one part of the garden from another. In a narrow garden, set the borders at right angles to the boundary walls. A border set against a path makes for easy maintenance, and the plants can visually soften the hard edge. Also try to site a perennial border where it can be seen from the house—ideally from the living or dining room.

Color schemes Late summer perennial borders tend to feature "hot" colors— yellows, oranges, and reds—and it's easy to create a whole border based on this naturally related color scheme. Multicolor borders are less limiting, and even a small clump of contrasting color can "lift" a scheme. There are plenty of cool blue and purple flowers which you can choose from, including aconites, *Gentiana asclepiadea,* and Michaelmas daisies. Easy-to-grow white flowers include baby's breath, *Achillea ptarmica,* and tall summer phlox (*Phlox paniculata*).

Late-flowering partners Old-fashioned shrubs, such as fuchsias, hydrangeas, and hybrid tea roses are all ideal for extras in the border, especially if they are tucked in here and there to fill out your newly planted beds. Other partners include annuals such as love-in-a-mist, sunflowers, and pot marigolds, which look good in a border. For high-level interest you could also train climbers against a wall-backed perennial border.

▲ Candy pink
This lovely pink flowering plant, Phlox paniculata "Pastorale" looks best planted in broad clumps in the middle or back of a border.

◄ Steely blue
Globe thistles (Echinops) contrast with yarrow, goldenrod, and bright red montbretia in a dense area of the perennial border.

---

tip

Border control
Sink corrugated iron sheets vertically into the ground between a perennial border and adjacent hedge to prevent the hedge roots from taking all the moisture and nutrients from the ground. Also lay a stepping-stone path down the center of wider borders, or at the back of front-facing ones, to make maintenance easier.

Popular late perennials

Blanketflower (*Gaillardia* cvs. [cultivars]) has yellow, flame, or wine-red flowers. It needs well-drained soil.

Coneflower (*Rudbeckia* cvs.) has golden-yellow daisylike blooms. A good plant for drying. It likes well-drained, fertile soil.

Garden chrysanthemum (Korean hybrids) has sprays of single or double flowers. Site in well-drained soil and in a sunny location.

Goldenrod (*Solidago* spp. and cvs.) has dense sprays of yellow flowers. It self-seeds rapidly and is invasive. It likes well-drained soil and sun.

Michaelmas daisy (*Aster* spp. and cvs.) comes in sprays of single or double

◄ *Cheerful coneflowers*
Rudbeckia *species include long-lasting, hardy annuals (shown here), biennials, and perennials.*

flowers in white, crimson, blue, or mauve. It is a potentially invasive plant which needs moist, well-drained soil and sun.

Montbretia (*Crocosmia* spp. and cvs.) has spikes of yellow or red funnel-shaped flowers. It likes well-drained soil.

Phlox (*Phlox* spp. and cvs.) has showy panicles of white, purple, or red flowers on tall stems. Likes sun or light shade.

Purple coneflower (*Echinaceas purpurea*) has purple or maroon daisylike flowers with orange centers. Thrives in well-drained soil.

Japanese anemone (*Anemone X hybrida*) has cup-shaped pink, white, or rosy-red flowers. It is invasive and thrives in rich, well-drained soil and light shade.

Sunflower (*Helianthus*) has deep-yellow single or double flowers.

Red-hot poker (*Kniphofia* spp. and cvs.) has erect spikes of tiny, pendent flowers in creamy white, yellow, orange, red, or bicolor. Needs well-drained soil.

Stonecrop (*Sedum* spp. and cvs.) has flat or domed heads of starry flowers, in red or brown; both types have fleshy leaves.

Yarrow (*Achillea* spp. and cvs.) has dense heads of tiny flowers in yellow, white, or pink and feathery, aromatic leaves.

◄ *Golden glory*
Goldenrod "Peter Pan," a vigorous, 3ft (90cm) high form, has unusual, horizontally branching flowers.

▼ *Compact choice*
"Golden Youth" and "Crimson Beauty" are 2ft (60cm) high dwarf forms of sneezewort.

Buying and caring for herbaceous plants

Buy pot-grown plants with healthy signs of growth. Choice of plants is greatest in fall and early spring.

Plant firmly in weed-free, well-dug, enriched soil. Plant where the soil is fairly dry, ideally in fall or spring. Plant in clumps of 3, 5, or 7 of each type, marking with labels.

Care: Water the plant regularly until established and thereafter in dry weather. Weed until plants knit, or grow together. Mulch annually in spring. Feed, stake, deadhead, and protect from pests and frost. Lift and divide every 3–5 years in spring. Replant young, outer sections of border in enriched soil.

COLORFUL AUTUMN LEAVES

As the summer cools off and fades into fall, why not let the vibrant colors of autumn leaves run riot in your garden?

While flowers are the traditional source of garden color, leaves with autumnal hues can be even more spectacular. They have more impact simply because the leaves are usually much larger than the flowers, and there are many more of them. You will find that the dazzling yellow, orange, scarlet, crimson, or mauve autumnal leaves of a substantial shrub or tree can light up a garden or even a whole landscape. This is particularly true in most parts of North America, where a sharp frost in the fall sets many trees ablaze with color.

The chief glory of the American autumn is, of course, the sugar maple, with its vivid red-orange foliage; but many other trees lend their distinctive hues to the autumn palette. The leaves of some dogwoods, such as *Cornus florida* and *Cornus kousa*, turn deep scarlet or wine-red, while the canoe birch (*Betula papyrifera*) turns a clear golden yellow. The delicate, feathery foliage of Japanese maples brings shades of gold, rust, or crimson into many a small garden.

Other plants, too, such as Virginia creeper, crimson glory vine, and some

▲ **Dense mound**
The slow-growing Acer palmatum *"Dissectum ornatum" has bronze-tinted leaves that turn a superb rich orange color in the fall.*

species of peony, provide autumnal color. Plants with colorful autumn foliage range widely in size, from dwarf heathers to stately sugar maple trees, which can grow up to 100ft (30m) tall. They also display variations in vigor, growth habit and leaf size, shape, color, and texture, as expected with such a wide range of garden plants, so be careful to choose a species that suits your garden and its capacity.

Choosing leaf colors

Autumn leaf color may last several weeks, but since some of the plants are vulnerable to the first blustery gale or hard frost, it can mean that some years your display may last for only a few days. It's especially important, therefore, to choose plants that will enhance the garden with other pleasing features, too, such as spring leaf color, pretty flowers, ornamental fruit or berries, colorful bark, or just simply the interesting silhouettes of their leafless winter branches.

Decide whether you want a tree or shrub, how much space is available, and the color or colors that best suit your garden's existing color scheme. Some autumn foliage plants, such as the lovely Japanese maples, are very slow-growing plants, while others, such as Norway maples, are fast growing, but will ultimately be too large for an ordinary-size garden. Some plants may also show different leaf colors depending on the type of soil. *Cercidiphyllum japonica*, for example, displays purple leaves on extremely acidic soil, but is more often seen with yellow leaves.

Some, such as birch, have light foliage, allowing a rich range of under-planting; others, such as beech, are dense and difficult to underplant. Some plants do best in sun, while others prefer light shade; some require humus-rich, acid soil, while others are tolerant of a wide range of soil types. It is important to buy plants that suit your soil type, so if you are in doubt, check your soil using a soil-testing kit.

Ideas for fall foliage plants

Most gardens are too small to warrant a border solely for fall interest, so it is a good idea to try to incorporate plants with autumn leaf color in mixed beds or borders, which will help to liven up these areas when the summer flowers fade. Autumn foliage plants that can be seen from the main windows of the house and plants that are lit by night lighting are especially effective.

Trees with autumn leaf color make excellent specimens and are great for siting in an open sweep of lawn, to give added color, or as the focal point in a smaller garden, particularly if placed in an island bed.

Fall colors are stunning against a dark background, such as a yew or holly hedge, or against the steel blue of a blue spruce. Alternatively, try placing the plants against a paler background—a whitewashed or adobe house or even a painted garden fence.

Train fall-foliage climbers to grow up tall trees or over unsightly garden

◀ **Compact brilliance**
Berberis thunbergii *comes in a wide variety of cultivars, all of which show subtle differences in leaf color. Here, the brilliant yellow is shown.*

▶ **Rainbow colors**
Acer palmatum *"Senkoki" leaves are yellow-orange in spring, green in summer, and pink, then finally yellow, toward the end of the fall season.*

▼ **Reliable color**
Eunymus alatus *is one of the most colorful and popular shrubs for fall color, offering lovely crimson leaves and bright orange seeds.*

sheds and garages, then interplant them with equally vigorous climbing roses or clematis, which will help to provide extended interest.

For a striking fall display you could include a few Japanese maples in a heather or dwarf conifer bed, which will give a range of contrasting colors, textures, and forms.

Another idea is to use harmonizing garden chrysanthemums, rockspray cotoneaster, or *Liriope muscari*, with spikes of tiny, purple, bead-like flowers as foreground planting for fall-foliage

shrubs. This will add extra color to the garden. Autumn crocus, especially yellow or purple varieties, and hardy cyclamen are good alternatives and will also add color to the scheme.

You can cool down fall foliage, if you wish, by placing it next to the icy silver leaves of artemisia, such as *A. schmidtiana* "Nana." The clear blue blooms of *Ceratostigma willmottianum*, Chinese plumbago, can also be used (in Zone 8) to complement the bright leaf colors; this scheme can look particularly effective on a clear, cool morning.

Popular fall foliage plants

These deciduous shrubs and trees are among those noted for their fall color.

Acer japonicum, the fullmoon maple, makes a large shrub or small tree, with seven-lobed leaves which turn crimson in fall. It likes moist soil, shade, and shelter.

Acer palmatum, the Japanese maple, includes many slow-growing cultivars making small, rounded trees, with five- or seven-lobed leaves and brilliant yellow, orange, or red fall color.

Amelanchier laevis, Allegheny serviceberry, has white flowers in spring, purple fruit, and orange-red autumn leaves.

Berberis thunbergii, the Japanese barberry, has small red or yellow leaves and scarlet berries in fall.

Cotinus coggygria, or smoke bush, has numerous cultivars with gray-green or purple foliage, turning red in fall, and delicate, plume-like flowers.

Cotoneaster horizontalis, the rockspray cotoneaster, has a distinctive, fishbone-like branching system and tiny leaves, which turn red in fall. It likes dry soil.

Eunymus alatus, winged spindle tree, makes a wide-spreading shrub, with crimson leaves and orange berries.

Fothergilla major has creamy white, petal-less flowers and yellow or red fall leaf color. Site in sun.

Parthenocissus quinquefolia, Virginia creeper, is crimson in fall, and has small black fruits in hot summers.

Rhododendron luteum, the deciduous azalea, has yellow flowers and crimson, purple, and orange fall leaf color.

Rhus typhina, the staghorn sumac, makes a flat-topped, wide-spreading shrub with pinnate leaves, orange-red in fall, and red seed cases. "Dissecta" has ferny leaves, yellow in fall.

Vitis coignetiae, the crimson glory vine, has large, rounded, heart-shaped leaves, which are bright red in autumn.

▲ Rockspray cotoneaster
The tiny leaves on the Cotoneaster horizontalis *are bright crimson in the fall, in glorious contrast to their orange-scarlet berries, which last into winter. Its branching pattern gives this plant the name "fishbone cotoneaster" in Britain.*

Buying and caring for foliage plants

Buy container-grown plants in fall or spring. Choose compact, well-balanced plants, true to type.

Plant firmly in weed-free soil, enriched if necessary. Stake or provide supports.

Site and soil depend on the plant chosen, but many prefer shelter and protection from frost and winds, and some dislike very hot sun.

Care: Weed and water until established, and thereafter in dry weather. Mulch annually and prune when dormant.

◄ Double value
Fothergilla major *has charming white bottle-brush-like flowers on totally bare branches during the spring season, then brilliant yellow and red autumn leaf colors. The plant thrives in full sun and likes peaty soil.*

WILD GARDENS

With the increasing interest in our environment and conserving our natural heritage, it's no wonder that wildflower gardening is becoming increasingly fashionable. Although you are unlikely to want to devote a whole garden to wildflowers, a small area left "wild" can provide welcome relief from the outsized, gaudy blooms that fill many gardens today.

Suitable plants

Native wildflowers are ideal, since they are naturally tough and self-sufficient, able to thrive and increase as long as the environment is broadly suitable. Also they provide food for bees, butterflies, and other forms of wildlife. Purists might insist on exclusively native wildflowers

for a wildflower garden, though some supposedly wild species, including perennial sweet pea and greater periwinkle, are actually garden escapes that naturalized centuries ago. There are also many wildflower species from other temperate climates, such as Japanese anemones, that look convincingly at home in American and European wildflower gardens.

A relaxed approach is best, combining native wildflowers with wild-looking garden plants, usually those with small, single flowers and a high proportion of leaf to flower. You can also include a few showy garden plants, with variegated or brightly colored leaves and large blooms, as long as they aren't visually overwhelming.

▲ The right approach
A meandering gravel path set in a slightly overgrown, informal mixture of wild and cultivated plants captures the spirit of wild gardening by recreating the haphazard diversity of meadows and country lanes.

Flowering annuals, biennials, perennials, and bulbs are important; flowering shrubs and non-flowering plants, such as ferns, or those with insignificant flowers, such as ivies or birch, provide a restful, cooling contrast. Match the choice of plants to the existing soil type. Alkaline soil, for example, is ideal for bluebell, wild thyme, and Chinese gentian; acid soil suits heather, rhododendron, and wild blueberry.

Types of wildflower gardens

You could devote your whole garden to wildflowers, but most people prefer to create a wildflower area, bed, or corner. In a large garden, it could be a self-contained, secluded retreat, such as the short leg of an L-shaped plot. In a small garden, it could be a patch next to a patio, or tucked unobtrusively away in a corner, under a tree, around a small pond or even over a pile of stones.

Woodland wildflower gardens Few flowers thrive in deep shade, but the light shade under birch, hazel, or dogwood is ideal for bluebells, wood anemone, primroses, hellebores, dogtooth violets, and foxgloves. The added height creates a pleasing sense of enclosure and, if the garden is overlooked, privacy. The flowers could grow in rough grass, or plants with dense foliage could be used to provide ground cover.

Meadow wildflower gardens A sunny area of rough grass, mowed twice a year, can display swathes of snowdrops in late winter; bluebells, daffodils, crocus, and grape hyacinths in spring; Queen Anne's lace, buttercups, and poppies in summer; and autumn crocus in fall. Damp areas of rough grass are ideal for fritillaries and ragged robin, or cuckooflower.

Waterside wildflower gardens If you have a permanently wet area, grow yellow flag iris, marsh marigolds, perennial forget-me-nots, and jack-in-the-pulpit.

How you arrange the plants is important. Large, informal clumps, overlapping at the edges and interweaving, are more natural-looking than rigidly set-out plants or the "one of each" approach. Avoid stretches of bare earth, which look cultivated rather than natural, and hard edges where the wildflower garden meets another surface. Gravel or lawn paths or meandering stepping-stones are ideal; if you have precast concrete paths, let the plants overspill to obscure the hard edge.

Source of wildflowers

It may be tempting to dig up flowers from the wild, but this can harm the local ecology and, in the case of protected plants, be illegal. Then, too, unless you know the timing and type of plant, you may well fail to transplant successfully. Digging up foxgloves in flower, for example, is pointless, since they are biennial, dying after flowering.

Specialist nurseries sell wildflowers grown from their own stock. Specialist seedsmen sell seeds, again collected from their own stock, of wildflowers in single type and mixed-seed packages, such as cornflowers, field poppies, or foxgloves, or mixed woodland wildflowers. Popular seed catalogs also have wildflower mixtures for sun and shade.

▲ Woodland clearing
Informal clumps of foxgloves, giant chives, and heathers fill a sunny clearing, set against a backdrop of mature trees.

▲ Harbingers of spring
*The common wild primrose (*Primula vulgaris*) has an innocent, fresh charm, ideal under deciduous trees, such as birch, hazel, or oak, or tucked under hedges.*

◄ Red, white, and blue
Clumps of field poppies, chamomile, and cornflowers create an eye-catching wild garden in miniature, with a border of heartsease and carefully controlled dandelions.

► Spring medley
*Daisies, buttercups, narcissi in variety, bluebells, speedwell, hardy geraniums, and the creamy-white sprays of false Solomon's seal (*Smilacina racemosa*) create a tapestry of spring color.*

Looking after wildflower gardens
As with any garden, it's best to start with weed-free, well-dug soil. You can also scatter seed on an existing rough lawn and take your chances, but the rate of germination will be lower. Whether you sow from seed or grow from plants, keep the area free of weeds, and water until the plants are established.

Thereafter, treat perennials and bulbs as you normally would, feeding in spring and lifting and dividing when over-crowded; the annuals and biennials should replace themselves.

One of the joys of wildflower gardening is allowing or even encouraging "happy accidents" to take place—self-seeded flowers popping up, perhaps in a

crack between paving slabs or at the base of a nearby shrub. What you can't do, however, is abandon a wildflower garden to its fate: nettles, docks, brambles, thistles, and other uninvited guests soon take over, and while they may encourage wildlife, there are far more attractive and much pleasanter ways of achieving the same result.

▲ Fruitful choice
The European wild strawberry (Fragaria vesca) has attractive evergreen leaves and dainty white flowers, as well as delicious and fragrant, if tiny, fruits.

▲ Colorful vignette
An old tree stump provides a natural focal point for Corsican hellebores, brunnera, with its forget-me-not-like flowers, and a stately clump of dark-blue-flowered alkanet.

▶ Cosmopolitan poppy
The so-called Welsh poppy, a cheerful, self-seeding, sun-loving perennial, grows wild through France, Portugal, Spain, and England, as well as Wales.

HERB GARDENS

Herbs add flavor to foods, provide extra scent and color in the garden, have cosmetic and medicinal uses, and are among the oldest cultivated plants, as fascinating and popular now as they were centuries ago.

Herbs range in size from creeping thyme, only 1in (2.5cm) tall, to bay, which grows to 60ft (18m) or more, and from weedy, but tasty, tarragon to lavender, as ornamental as it is fragrant.

Herbs can be annual, biennial, perennial, or woody. Most have modest flowers and foliage, but some, including borage, nasturtium, and chives, have showy blooms, and others, such as sage and balm, have strikingly colored leaves. Many herbs attract bees and butterflies, bringing additional color and interest to a garden.

Formal herb gardens, with herbs set out in geometric beds and bounded by gravel paths, are traditional; but herbs can also be grown informally, in clumps in perennial or mixed borders. Compact herbs, such as parsley and dwarf lavender, make excellent edging plants. Containerized herb gardens, with individual or mixed herbs grown in flower pots, stone sinks, or tubs, are perfect for patios. For city dwellers, a window box can easily become the perfect herb garden in miniature.

Popular herbs

Basil (*Ocimum basilicum*). Sweet basil is a half-hardy annual with shiny green leaves and is perfect with tomato dishes. It grows up to 2ft (60cm) tall. It needs sun, shelter, and regular pinching out to keep it compact.

Bay (*Laurus nobilis*). Often grown as a standard or small, pyramid-shaped bush, this evergreen can reach 60ft (18m) in the wild, but is slow-growing in pots. Use the leaves in bouquets garnis or to flavor fish dishes, stews, and sauces.

Bee Balm (*Monarda didymu*). This herbaceous perennial grows up to 3ft (90cm) tall and has striking red hooded flowers. Its pungent leaves can be used, like sage or rosemary, in red meat and poultry dishes. Like the related species *M. fistulosa* (wild bergamot), it is an excellent plant for perennial borders.

▲ A break with tradition
This herb garden, set in a paved area, features many old favorites: chives, sage, thyme, golden marjoram, lavender cotton, and rosemary. It is given a modern touch with the spider plant, complete with spidery runners, filling an old-fashioned Ali Baba-style pot.

Borage (*Borago officinalis*). This hardy annual, 1–2ft (30–60cm) tall, has intensely blue flowers. It's used to garnish summer drinks, and its leaves

parsley

add flavor to salads and soups. A self-seeder, it is ideal in a wild garden.

Chervil (*Anthriscus cerefolium*). A delicate, ferny annual or biennial 1ft (30cm) tall, chervil has a peppery flavor which is strongest fresh, used in soup, poultry, or salad dishes. If it is planted in a sunny, sheltered spot, you can harvest its leaves all winter long.

Chives (*Allium schoenoprasum*). With their tidy, grassy leaves, mild onion flavor, and pincushion flowers, chives rate a place in any garden. Ordinary chives are 6in (15cm) tall; giant chives, twice that. They make a perfect edging plant. Finely chopped, they are used as a garnish in salads and in potato dishes, and to flavor cottage cheese.

Coriander, or cilantro (*Coriandrum sativum*). This feathery-leaved annual grows to a height of 1–2ft (30–60cm) and bears small white flowers in summer. The peppery leaves and spicy seeds are used to flavor many Asian, Middle Eastern, and Latin American dishes.

Dill (*Anethum graveolens*). This easy annual grows up to 3ft (90cm) tall and has delicate, feathery leaves and aromatic seeds, perfect with fish, eggs, tomatoes, and in pickling. Its flat yellow flower heads enhance mixed borders.

Fennel (*Foeniculum vulgare*). Similar to dill in looks and flavor, but perennial and growing up to 6ft (1.8m) tall, fennel is handsome enough for ornamental use.

Garlic (*Allium sativum*). Its distinctively strong flavor enhances meat, vegetables, and salad dressings. Easy to grow, single cloves, planted in spring, yield complete heads by late summer.

Hyssop (*Hyssopus officinalis*). This woody perennial, up to 2ft (60cm) high, has spikes of tiny, tubular flowers in pink, mauve or white, and is much loved

by bees and butterflies. Its bitter leaves flavor stews, fruit pies, and stuffings. It is a traditional edging plant for herb and knot gardens.

Lemon balm (*Melissa officinalis*). The lemony scent attracts bees, and its leaves flavor salads, drinks, and poultry dishes. A tough, self-seeding hardy perennial, it grows up to 2ft (60cm) tall. The gold variegated form "Aurea" is prettier and less invasive.

Lovage (*Levisticum officinale*). The leaves of this coarse-looking perennial, which grows up to 6ft (1.6m) tall, add a sharp, taste to soups and savory dishes. Unless you have a huge herb garden, confine it to a semi-wild patch.

Marjoram Sweet marjoram (*Origanum majorana*) is the most popular and flavorful species. Usually grown as a half-hardy annual, it has tiny clusters of pink flowers. Pot marjoram (*O. onites*), a perennial, is hardier but coarser fla-

▲ *Paved herb gardens*
Chives, various thymes, marjorams, and heartsease thrive in the open joints of brick paving. Sage-filled terracotta pots complete the picture.

vored. "Aurea," the golden form of wild marjoram (*O. vulgare*), is often sold as an ornamental, but its leaves are equally useful in the kitchen. All grow to 1ft (30cm) tall.

Mint Spearmint (*Mentha spicata*), with spear-shaped leaves; variegated apple mint (*M. suaveolens* "Variegata"), and the wooly-leaved *M. rotundifolia* "Bowles" are all perennial. They grow to 18–24in (45–60cm) tall and prefer moist, rich soil. They can be invasive and are best grown in containers, or in buckets sunk in the ground. Mint jelly with lamb, and fresh mint with peas or new potatoes are traditional.

dill

Parsley (*Petroselinium crispum*). The most popular herb, parsley enhances virtually any savory dish. A biennial, sometimes grown as an annual, it grows 8in–2ft (20–60cm) tall in plain and fern-leaved or moss-curled forms. The latter make an attractive edging.

Rosemary (*Rosmarinus officinalis*). This hardy, evergreen, somewhat sprawling shrub usually grows up to 3ft (90cm) tall. It has needle-like, intensely aromatic leaves and small blue flowers. It stands container growing and pruning well and is used to flavor rich meats and vinegars.

Sage (*Salvia officinalis*). Besides the gray-leaved species, there are varieties such as "Icterina," which is variegated gold and green; "Purpurea," which has handsome, purple-flushed leaves; and "Tricolor," which is pink, white, purple, and gray. All are nearly hardy shrubs, benefiting from annual pruning in spring. Sage is traditionally used in turkey stuffing, but poultry and cheese can also be flavored with this herb.

Tarragon (*Artemisia dracunculus*). A floppy, coarse perennial, 2ft (60cm) tall, tarragon has a fresh, tart taste and is used in fish, chicken, and seafood dishes, salads and sauces. Grow the French, not the inferior Russian, tarragon.

Thyme Common thyme (*Thymus vulgaris*) is a wide-spreading shrub, 1ft (30cm) tall. Lemon thyme (*T. citriodorus*) is lemon-scented, gold-leaved in the form "Aureus," silver-variegated in "Silver Queen." Wild thyme (*T. serpyllum*) is a creeping perennial, useful for herb paths; there are many named forms, with white, pink, or crimson flowers. Thyme is used to flavor red meat, poultry, and vegetable dishes.

▲ **Mixed medley**
Chives, lemon balm, and angelica are joined in their box-edged bed by Euphorbia lathyris, *a cottage-garden plant reputed to discourage moles.*

▼ **Herbal tapestry**
Purple sage and silver lavender combine to create a study in aromatic foliage, enlivened by bright yellow tansy flowers.

lemon balm

Care and cultivation
Site: Most herbs, especially ones with Mediterranean origins, need full sun, shelter, and well-drained soil to develop their essential oils. In pots, use potting soil with grit or sand added, and always place drainage material in the bottom.
Buy: You can grow most herbs from seed, but unless you need large numbers, buy young, pot-grown plants. Plant out in spring in weed-free soil, firm well, and water until established. Thereafter, water open-grown herbs only in extended drought; water herbs in pots whenever the soil looks and feels dry. Parsley and chervil, however, need regular watering in summer.
Care: If growing herbs solely for flavor, nip off the flower buds; this also helps to extend the life of parsley, chervil, and other biennials. Most people, however, are prepared to forego culinary perfection so they can enjoy the flowers.

◄ *Scented seat*
In this sheltered garden, roses, pinks, and herbs provide a heady fragrance.

◄ *Sages in variety*
Clumps of variegated, purple, and ordinary sage edge this border filled with fennel, thyme, and oregano.

Harvesting

For fresh herbs, pick only a few leaves, as you need them, from any one plant, so that it remains strong. For preserving, you can harvest more generously; but again, if you want it to continue thriving, leave at least half the plant intact.

Choose a dry, sunny morning and, ideally, plants which are just about to flower. Hang small, loose bunches upside down in a dry, airy spot, out of direct sunlight. When leaves are bone-dry and papery, strip them from the stems, crumble, and store in airtight containers. Herbs can also be dried in a low oven with the door left ajar, or in a microwave set to low for up to five minutes.

Parsley, chervil, and chives freeze better than they dry; chop the leaves, pack in icecube trays, fill with water, and freeze. Once frozen, pack in freezer bags. Alternatively, chop the leaves, place in freezer bags, seal, and label. However, they may lose some of their taste in the process.

ORNAMENTAL VEGETABLES

Although often grown in an out-of-the-way plot, garden vegetables can be as attractive as any ornamental plant. Scarlet runner beans, for example, were first grown in Europe for their vivid blooms and elegant foliage, and tomatoes were included for the decorative quality of their colorful fruit. It was later that these plants were recognized for their food value. In today's smaller gardens, growing plants that are both edible and ornamental is a creative way to make maximum use of space and get the best of both worlds. As edging,

infill, or as a screen, in the open ground, or in containers, decorative vegetables can provide color, interest, and tasty crops. It's just a question of looking at them with "new" eyes, assessing their appearance as well as their purpose.

Contrast is a strong part of decorative pattern, and the well-planned positioning of "ordinary" vegetables, such as tall, arching leeks and lacy carrot foliage, can produce surprisingly ornamental effects, though they may not be considered particularly decorative in their own right.

▲ *Sweet perfection*
Sweet, or bell, peppers are ideal for container growing and carry ripe yellow, red, or purple fruits, according to variety. To encourage the peppers to grow, it's a good idea to spray the flowers and young fruit with water. The plant is notably tender to frost, so it's best to overwinter indoors.

◄ **Globe artichoke**
The leaf scales of the flower are eaten before they form thistles.

▲ **Golden glow**
Yellow zucchini add extra color to a garden, as do many other squashes.

Choosing decorative vegetables

Decide if you want to harvest the crop or just enjoy its appearance. Like any plants, vegetables should be chosen to suit your soil and aspect. Some varieties are specifically for early or late growing. Always check the packet.

Consider height, growth habit, and color in relation to the setting. Some, such as lettuce, are quick-growing; others like Brussels sprouts, are slow, taking two growing seasons to reach maturity; and a few are perennial, reappearing year after year.

Think about the display season. Most ornamental vegetables are at their best in late spring and summer, but flowering kale gives winter interest. If you can grow plants from seed, the choice is larger than if you buy young plants from garden centers, though the latter give quicker results.

Decorative ideas

Formal or **informal** Ornamental fruit and vegetable gardens, or *potagers*, traditionally have formal geometric plans, with plants set out in quilt-like patterns. You can turn a vegetable plot into a *potager* with slightly raised beds, diagonal or right-angled paths, and an urn, birdbath, or fruit tree in the center. Herbs and a few "real" ornamentals, such as roses, add to the effect. Curly or red lettuce makes pretty edging to a flowerbed, and leafy vegetables can be grown in clumps.

Plant partners Grow globe artichokes in a silver and gray border, with artemisias, lychnis, or *Stachys byzantina*; or ruby chard with purple-leaved sage and ajuga. Interplant ornamental vegetables with herbs, such as moss-curled parsley.

► **Exotic "blooms"**
Flowering cabbages and kales produce flower-like rosettes in a stunning range of color combinations.

▼ **Curiosity value**
Odd rather than beautiful, kohlrabi is quick-growing. It likes alkaline soil.

Use ornamental foliage corn as dot plants, with pelargoniums, in formal bedding, or in subtropical schemes with honey-flower (*Melianthus major*).

Mix and match Buy mixed seed packets, such as mixed lettuce or gourds, for a multicolor, multi-texture effect.

Support ideas Grow trailing gourds or scarlet runner beans up bamboo tepees as focal points in a border. Trained up netting, they can conceal ugly walls. Grow scarlet runners over arches.

Container options Grow mini-tomatoes, peppers, or flowering kale in pots on a patio garden, or in a window box.

Finishing touches Use the colorful leaves in flower arrangements.

Popular ornamental vegetables

Asparagus is a perennial needing full sun and well-drained soil. Early shoots are harvested; later ones grow out into fern-like plumes. Grow from seed.

Cucurbits (*Cucurbitaceae*), all half-hardy annuals, include pumpkins, marrows, squashes, and ornamental gourds. Sow under glass; transplant in late spring.

Florence fennel is an annual grown for its base, though its foliage is also tasty. Grow in hot sun and sandy soil.

Flowering cabbages and **kales** are biennials grown as annuals, forming rosettes of frilled leaves. Sow under glass and transplant in late spring. Grow in rich soil and in full sun; kales can winter outdoors in temperatures above 32°F (0°C).

Globe artichokes are perennials with silver leaves and stately thistles. Grow in sun and well-drained soil. Grow from seed or buy young plants.

Kohlrabi is a biennial grown as an annual for its stem base. Sow outdoors in sun and well-drained, poor soil.

Lettuce is a quick-growing annual with many varieties, some red, others cut-leafed. Loose-leaf types, such as "Salad -bowl," are picked leaf by leaf. Sow all season or buy young plants. Sow under glass for early crops, outdoors from mid-spring on. Grow in well-drained soil and sun, light shade in hot summers.

Ornamental corn is an annual, 4–5ft (1.2–1.5m) tall, with multicolored leaves in "Quadricolor," green-and-white-striped in the dwarf "Gracillima Variegata." Grow in well-drained soil.

▲ **Filigree foliage**
Florence fennel, a close relative of the herb, is grown for its swollen base; its foliage can also be used.

Scarlet runner beans are half-hardy annuals with attractive foliage and red, white, or bicolor, sweet pea flowers. Sow outdoors after the last frost.

Sweet peppers, or **bell peppers**, are bushy, half-hardy annuals with green fruit which turns red, yellow, or purple when ripe. Sow under glass and plant after the last frost. Grow in sun and well-drained soil.

Swiss chard is an annual with green leaves and scarlet, yellow, white, or orange stalks. "Rainbow" has multicolored stalks.

Tomatoes are half-hardy annuals, needing sun and rich, well-drained soil. Sow under glass and plant out. Bush varieties with red, yellow, or striped fruit, and cherry tomatoes, with masses of tiny fruit, are especially attractive.

Buying and caring for ornamental vegetables
Buy seeds in late winter; check the sell-by date. Young plants are often sold in catalogs.
Site vegetables in a sunny, sheltered position with well-drained soil. Apply fertilizer before sowing or planting.
Sow thinly in trays under glass, in a seed bed or *in-situ*. Thin and transplant as necessary. Plant young plants firmly, spacing them according to instructions on the seed packet, and water in well.
Care: Keep watered and weeded. Mulch, feed, and spray against pests as necessary. Support tall-growing varieties. Harvest vegetables such as beans regularly.

Understanding squashes

Pumpkins, other squashes and ornamental gourds are all half-hardy annuals belonging to the cucurbit family. They are technically fruit, since they contain seeds, but are usually cooked as vegetables, although pumpkin pie is a famous exception.

Edible squashes are usually divided into bush and trailing varieties; the former are better for small gardens. Small summer squashes, including scalloped and curved-neck varieties, are harvested and eaten young. Winter squashes, including buttercups, hubbards, butternuts, and acorn squash, are harvested in fall.

Small ornamental gourds come in a variety of shapes. Large or calabash gourds are generally club- or bottle-shaped, although Turk's cap is turban-shaped. To dry ornamental gourds, cut when mature leaving the stalk intact. Sponge off soil with dilute disinfectant, and prick a tiny hole in each end for ventilation. Hang up or place on wire racks in a cool, airy spot to dry. It can take months. If the seeds rattle when shaken, the gourd is ready. Varnish, if desired.

▲ Scalloped choice
"Custard White" is a non-keeping summer variety of squash. Harvest young, and bake, boil, or braise.

▲ Turk's cap
A form of calabash, this inedible, ornamental gourd needs hot summers to reach its full size.

▶ Fall favorite
Pumpkin is a long-keeping squash, much used for Thanksgiving and Halloween decorations.

GARDEN ACCESSORIES

Add a touch of class and a sense of permanence to your garden with a selection of traditional or imaginative statues and fancy ornaments.

With the wide range of reasonably priced accessories available at virtually every garden center, it's easy to add instant interest to your garden, however small. In addition to purely ornamental accessories, such as statues, functional garden items, such as birdbaths, furniture, and even flowerpots can act as garden ornaments, so always try to choose practical items with this in mind.

Garden accessories range from tiny stone frogs to larger-than-life Grecian-style statues. They come in a wide variety of materials. At the luxury end of the market are those made of stone. An imitation called "cast stone"—essentially concrete—provides a similar effect at a much lower cost. Some of this is colored to suggest different kinds of stone, either with a pigment added to the mix or, more inexpensively, with paint. Hardwoods such as teak and iroko and softwoods such as cedar and pine are used especially for garden furniture. They should be treated with a preservative. Metals used include aluminum, cast iron, and brass. Fiberglass and plastic are other often-used materials.

The garden accessories themselves can be either permanent or movable; formal or informal; imposing or light-hearted and humorous; traditional or unusual, even eccentric; lifelike or stylized; subtle or bold and brash—the choice is yours.

Choosing garden accessories

Keep in mind your garden's size and style and the color of any large areas of paving or walls. Consider, too, the setting and any nearby buildings. New garden accessories should fit in comfortably with existing ones.

Before buying an accessory, decide where it is to go. A few large accessories generally look better than a plethora of smaller ones. Pairs of identical accessories, such as statues on either side of a front door or gate, can be very effective if you want to add formality.

Buy the best quality you can afford, since most garden accessories are long-term investments. Do some comparison shopping for offers, and ask about guarantees. Genuine antique garden accessories are expensive and also vulnerable to theft; good-quality reproductions are more than adequate.

Consider any special transportation needs and whether special foundations or fixings will be required. Fountains will need a nearby electricity supply. Make sure that there is adequate access to the garden for larger items.

◀ **Leafy retreat**
Where you put the new statue will affect the style of the garden. Here, a stone child peers out shyly from its fragrant, shadowy setting of honeysuckle and viburnum, adding an element of secrecy to the garden. For a bolder effect the statue could be positioned in a more visible place.

Siting garden accessories

You can site an accessory where it is seen to the maximum—in the center of a front lawn, visible from most main rooms in the house; or almost hide it—placing a stone tortoise under a hosta leaf, for example. There is also an infinite number of variations in between.

Corners, flowerbeds, and borders are good positions, since they create an automatic setting. A change of level, such as at the top or bottom of a flight of steps or where two paths meet, is also a good place for an ornament.

Try to site pale accessories against a dark backdrop, such as a hedge or garden wall, or in a naturally shady spot. Dark accessories, such as lead plant troughs, look best against a pale setting—a white or cream wall, for example.

Popular garden accessories

Statues are probably the most popular garden ornaments. They range from plastic, concrete, or painted plaster garden gnomes and windmills, to stately stone obelisks and Grecian or Roman gods and goddesses. Statues of children and animals—dogs, cats, cranes, hedgehogs, pigs or mythological unicorns, or griffins—are particularly enchanting. For additional grandeur, a statue can be placed on a stone plinth or act as a fountain for use with a pump.

Flowerpots range from simple to ornate in design, and from very small to mammoth in size. Generally, the larger the pot, the more effective it is as a focal point. The degree of ornateness has relatively little relation to impact: quite simple pots can have a stately elegance, and over-ornamented pots may look very fussy.

Fountains can be freestanding or attached to a wall, in styles ranging from a pure spout of water breaking the surface of the pond to ornate statuary with fish, frogs, or lions spouting water from their mouths. For very small gardens, or where young children use the garden, there are trickle fountains which send a gentle flow of water over a millstone, to be collected beneath and recirculated by means of a hidden valve and pump.

Furniture should combine comfort and beauty, whatever its style. You can choose matching suites, or mix-and-match furniture with a common theme, perhaps adding bright color with cushions, tablecloths, or big umbrellas.

Wall plaques, such as cherubs' heads, grotesques, or lion's masks are ideal for gardens where space is at a premium, and the plaque can double as a fountain if you choose one with an open mouth.

Finials, such as stone pineapples or globes, were traditionally used to decorate walls, but can be used as accessories in their own right, set among ground-cover plants or next to a garden pool.

Sundials made of bronze, brass, or slate and set horizontally on raised stone plinths in the ground, or fixed vertically to a wall, add a timeless quality, even when gray, cloudy days prevent their effectiveness.

Birdhouses and feeders can be free-standing or hung, and come in a great variety of styles, from the simple to the elaborate. Birdbaths are generally stone or concrete, available on pedestals or as ground-level basins.

Objets trouvés, including old wheelbarrows, wagon wheels, chimney pots, horse troughs, agricultural tools, even old horseshoes nailed to a tool-house door, can become garden accessories, depending on your imagination and taste. Use too many, though, and your garden may start to look like a junkyard.

Natural objects, such as handsomely shaped large pebbles and rocks, can be used as focal point accessories—in oriental gardens they have long been used to symbolize mountains and other land formations. Large, sun-bleached pieces of driftwood or statuesque sections of tree trunks can also be used as garden ornaments, with plants trained over them for a subtle effect.

▼*Triple show*
Three terracotta pots in graduating sizes create a pretty, tiered effect, filled with summer blooms.

▲Practical and pretty
This elegant metal bench acts as a focal point set against the dark brickwork. A hybrid tea rose, "Adelaide D'Orléans," adds the finishing touch. By training the rose around the bench you can create a scented seat.

◄ Classical theme
A smiling cherub holds aloft a spouting dolphin, in a traditional-style fountain which is small enough for almost any garden. Similar statues can be bought from many good garden centers.

▼ Sunny spot
For an unusual effect, you can plant accessories in the garden. Here, a ground-level sundial nestles among contrasting cobblestones, interplanted with alpines and perennials.

◄ **Faithful friend**
A stone hound-dog sits patiently by the entrance to a small courtyard-type garden, surrounded by a low brick wall, as if guarding it faithfully to ward off any unwelcome guests.

► **Permanent pair**
A delightful pair of bronze geese combines timeless permanence with charming informality, as they graze together contentedly on the carefully mown lawn.

▼ **Clever re-use**
An old Victorian-Gothic chimney pot makes an excellent focal point filled with mixed geraniums and lobelias, and it provides a perfect place for the family cat to sit.

Garden accessories and plants

Garden accessories are natural partners for plants, their timeless quality contrasting with the seasonal variations in the garden.

A small statue or wooden bench looks lovely if placed near a tall yew, beech, holly, or hornbeam hedge. The hedging works as a backdrop, and its branches can be trained to act as extensions, wrapping around the garden ornament, like an armchair.

You could surround a planted urn by growing the same color and type of plant around the base: a petunia-filled urn surrounded by petunias, for example, or, in spring, a daffodil- or tulip-filled urn surrounded by golden dancing daffodils or colorful tulips.

Train ivy or clematis up and over a statue or along the back of a permanent garden bench. This was a popular idea in Victorian gardens. Plant stone shepherdesses' baskets with houseleeks (*Sempervivum*).

In a paved courtyard garden, you could make a special central feature by placing an ornate statue in a square or circular flowerbed.

tip

Frosty weather
Always check whether a terracotta accessory is frost-proof before you buy it. If it isn't, or if you are in doubt, move it under cover over the winter months.

2
THE POTTED COUNTRY GARDEN

CHOOSING CONTAINER PLANTS

A tiny garden or balcony is the perfect setting for tubs, troughs, and hanging baskets of cascading foliage and flowering plants.

The lack of a "proper" garden needn't cramp your gardening style at all, since there are hundreds of varieties of hardy plants that thrive in containers and can transform even the bleakest-looking balcony or backyard into an intimate, leafy retreat. As with ordinary gardens, pots of tender plants like fuchsias, pelargoniums, or geraniums, and petunias can create a vibrant seasonal display from early summer into mid-fall, followed by early-flowering pansies and snowdrops and then the wallflowers, daffodils, tulips, forget-me-nots, and hyacinths of spring.

There are trees, shrubs, climbers, perennials, biennials, annuals, and bulbs suitable for balcony and backyard gardens, ranging from miniature alpines, 1in (2.5cm) or less in height to wisteria, 30ft (9m) or taller. Because most backyards and balconies are small, it takes fewer plants to create a dense, lush effect, but it is especially important not to waste space on temperamental plants or on permanent plants whose display period is brief. Far better to choose a plant whose foliage and, possibly, flowers will provide color and pleasure throughout the seasons.

▼ *High and dry*
This plant-filled balcony offers a private retreat and a delightful overview of the garden beneath.

Balcony and backyard plants

Formal or informal The architectural styles of the house, garden walls, if any, and paving usually set the tone. Clipped topiary box or bay trees in square white Versailles tubs, pairs or rows of identical, plant-filled pots, and mono-chromatic color schemes can emphasize formality, while the pleasant chaos of intermingling, multicolored plants in clusters of various-sized pots is more informal, like a cottage garden.

Grouping plants Try a split-level approach, planting low-growing bulbs, annuals, or bedding plants at the base of a tub containing a permanent shrub, such as bay or box; or place ground-level containers below a window box, hanging baskets, or narrow plant table; or use a Victorian-style tiered plant stand for an instant, multilevel display. Corners are ideal for tight plant groups, providing shelter and a natural frame. Grouping plants around a door or gate is effective. Where steps lead from a balcony down into the garden, train clematis, wisteria, or honeysuckle up the railings.

◄ *Two-tier show*
Rooftop clematis and ground-level box topiary, fuchsias, ferns, and lavender set the scene for dinner in this pretty brick-paved backyard.

Choosing plants

Personal taste counts, but try also to match the plants to the aspect and exposure of your balcony or backyard. You can easily meet the soil needs by choosing the correct potting mixture— a nutrient-rich, loam-based soil for most plants and an acidic mixture for lime-haters such as camellias and rhodo-dendrons. Backyards surrounded by solid walls are sheltered and (unless north-facing) create sun traps when the sun is shining. So they are mild enough in winter for semi-hardy plants such as pelargonium and passion flower to survive outdoors all year round in the warmer temperature zones of the U.S.

Plants for balconies need careful thought, since they can be very exposed to winds. You can line balcony railings with clear plastic to act as a windbreak.

Aim for a high proportion of evergreen plants to provide basic, year-round cover; most evergreens are also shade-tolerant. Try, too, to include as many climbers as possible, since there is usually more wall than ground space available. If you are unsure whether a specific plant will thrive in a container, inquire before buying.

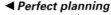

Plant combinations In a sunny, sheltered spot, plant a potted herb garden of lavender, bay, rosemary, tarragon, and chives with variegated forms of sage and thyme. Or concentrate on gray and silver-leaved plants such as *Senecio cineraria*, lavender, rue, and lavender cotton, with succulents such as house-leek (*Sempervivum*) for contrast in form. In a shady backyard or balcony, combine ferns, hostas, ivies, and, in summer, impatiens and flowering tobacco plants.

Virtually any color combination used in the open garden is suitable, but white or pastel flowers and green and white variegated foliage are especially effective for adding sparkle to shade; yellow variegated foliage tends to color best in sun, where deep, rich flower colors are also displayed to best advantage.

Ornaments Balcony and courtyard gardens are ideal for displaying stone statuary, a collection of handsome waterwashed stones, or even seashells. Don't forget walls, for wall plaques, fountains, or flat-backed half baskets.

A plant-framed mirror can be delightful, increasing the sense of space and light. Remember that any containers are also on show. Choose attractive terracotta, wood, or reconstituted stone models; on balconies, if loading is a problem, choose lightweight fiberglass. You can either grow the plants directly in them or plant them in a concealed inner pot.

Popular types
Annuals Petunia, lobelia, nasturtium, flowering tobacco plant, ageratum, butterfly flower, African and French marigolds, dahlia, sunflower, morning glory—virtually any annual will do. After the last frost, buy trays or pots of compact plants just coming into flower or in bud but with color showing. Avoid overcrowded plants or those with wilted or yellow leaves.
Biennials Choose wallflowers, pansies, polyanthus, forget-me-nots, English daisies, sweet William, or Canterbury bells. Buy compact, leafy plants in fall or, as a more costly alternative, plants with well-formed flower buds in winter or spring.

◄ *Perfect planning*
An arch, trellis, a statue, fine pots, and a small pond bring style to this garden.

► *Vertical element*
The lush foliage of a trained grapevine contrasts with cheerful annuals in this sunny backyard garden.

◄ *Prodigal pots*
Plant-filled terracotta pots, including a huge, dramatic Ali Baba-style pot, enhance a narrow, wooden deck balcony. Planting white impatiens around the bases of the standard fuchsias makes the most of the limited space.

tip

Instant walls
If a balcony is part of a continuous row, fix a trellis at each end for climbing plants and to screen off your neighbors. When a backyard is surrounded by a low wall, fix trellis panels to the top for increased privacy and plant support.

▲ Tree tops
A sheltered, leafy balcony makes an ideal spot for dining out in balmy weather. All the different leaves have a cooling effect, casting a dappled shade over the table and chairs. A potted pelargonium adds a touch of color.

▶ Regal display
The fiery blooms of crown imperial (Fritillaria imperialis) fill a small patch of open soil at the base of a wall-trained vine. If paving a patio, leave out a few slabs for planting lavender or thyme.

Caring for balcony and backyard plants
Plant firmly in containers of loam-based potting mixture, with plenty of drainage material in the base. If planting in the open ground, enrich the soil first with well-rotted compost or leaf mold, checking that all the plants need similar conditions for healthy growth.
Stake standards such as fuchsias, and provide support for climbers; even self-clinging climbers such as ivy need initial support.
Water regularly, especially in hot weather. The smaller the container, the more frequently it needs watering—daily in long, dry spells. Hose down in very hot weather, using a nozzle with a fine spray.
Feed every week from late spring until late summer during the growing period, using granules or dilute liquid fertilizer, according to manufacturer's instructions.
Protect from long, hard frosts by wrapping containers in blankets, bracken, or sacking, or move into a cool, bright spot indoors. Also protect from slugs with slug pellets and spray against aphids at the first sign of trouble.
Discard annuals and biennials after flowering. Discard tender bedding plants in fall, or move to a cool, bright spot indoors to overwinter. Lift and dry off spring bulbs, then store over summer and replant in fall. Container-grown shrubs rarely need pruning, but if necessary, prune deciduous ones when dormant and evergreens once or twice in summer, as necessary.

Tender bedding plants Choose verbenas, marguerites, fuchsias, and zonal or ivy-leaved pelargoniums for sun, and fuchsias, wishbone flower, impatiens, and scented-leaved pelargoniums for shade. Buy leafy plants with plenty of flower buds, after the last frost.
Bulbs Choose snowdrops, netted iris (Iris reticulata), and winter aconites; hyacinths, grape hyacinths, tulips, crocus, daffodils, and narcissi for spring; lilies for summer and autumn-flowering crocus and cyclamen. Plant plump, disease-free, dormant bulbs in fall, cyclamen in summer, or pots of bulbs coming into flower in season.

Perennials Choose tough, tolerant plants such as acanthus, hellebore, hosta, hardy geranium, euphorbia, periwinkle, bergenia, hybrid daylilies, California poppy, or lamb's ears, with attractive foliage as well as flowers. Fill a container with just one type, or group several different types in one container.
Shrubs Traditional backyard shrubs include shade-tolerant camellia, mountain laurel, fatsia, fuchsia, holly, rhododendron, skimmia, pieris, sweet pepperbush, and eunymous and sun-loving *Senecio cineraria*, rose, cordyline, lavender cotton, and lavender.
Trees compact enough for container

growing include bay, Japanese maple, golden honey locust (*Gleditsia triacanthos* "Sunburst"), and the hardy mimosa (*Albizia julibrissin* "E.H. Wilison"). Dwarf weeping trees, such as the golden weeping willow (*Salix alba* "Tristis"), make attractive focal points, as does the corkscrew willow (*S. matsudana* "Tortuosa").
Climbers For sun, choose wisteria, summer jasmine, *Clematis armandii*, passion flower, or climbing roses. For light shade, choose clematis, winter-flowering jasmine, or honeysuckle, and for deep shade, variegated ivy or climbing hydrangea.

PLANTS IN POTS

Growing plants in containers is a simple and effective way of giving a country look to your garden, whatever its size. You can move your pots and containers around to catch the sun at different times of year or to create different effects. Be as ambitious as you like: using a large variety of pots and containers, you can create an instant garden with year-round interest, with shrubs, herbs, annuals, and perennials in a number of combinations; or you can simply opt for a pair of matching tubs filled with colorful summer plants to stand beside the front door. Whatever you choose, there are a few basic rules that you should follow for successful container planting.

The container
You can grow plants in practically anything, from commercially produced pots, urns, and tubs in terracotta, stone, wood, and plastic, to improvised homemade containers.

When choosing containers, keep in mind the eventual size of your plants; shrubs will need plenty of room for their roots, whereas annuals can thrive in much smaller pots. Remember that a fully planted container will be very heavy, so either put your pot in its final position before planting or keep your containers to a manageable size.

Drainage
All containers need good drainage, so drill several holes in the bottom, and put in a layer of pebbles or broken pots at least 1in (2.5cm) deep; a drainage layer one-third of the depth of the pot will do no harm.

If your container is made of wood, standing it on some bricks will help to prevent it from rotting. A layer of pebbles under any container will improve drainage in a wet winter, and in summer you can dampen the pebbles and they'll help keep the soil in the tub moist.

Cover the drainage layer with a piece of sacking to prevent the soil from washing out, then fill the container right up to the top with potting mixture; one with a neutral or near-neutral pH (neither acidic nor alkaline) suits most plants, but rhododendrons, camellias, and azaleas need a lime-free mixture. The mixture should be at least as deep as that in the container the plant was in previously.

Feeding and watering
There is a risk of overfeeding plants in containers, so be careful to follow the manufacturer's instructions on dosage for your particular plants; slow-release organic fertilizers are safest. Container-grown plants tend to dry out much more quickly than they would in the open ground, and annuals especially need frequent watering in hot weather.

Plants in pots are subject to extremes of temperature, so in winter you may need to wrap the pots in old blankets to protect the roots from frost, or even bring them indoors.

◄ **Instant color**
*Brighten up the corner of a patio or the area around the front door with a selection of pots of vibrant-colored plants. In front of a mellow stone wall, fleshy red and white tuberous begonias (*Begonia x tuberhybrida*) contrast beautifully with white petunias and a tiny container of mixed lobelia.*

◄ **A profusion of pots**
A range of pots and containers in different sizes and shapes can be used to great effect—in this way you can mix plants that don't necessarily thrive in the same kind of soil. Here deep pink petunias mingle with crimson tobacco plants in a terracotta pot, the blooms of Lychnis coronaria *in the stone trough blend with fuchsias and petunias in other pots; and the dark, shiny leaves of the stately agapanthus provide a background.*

Maintenance

Frequent deadheading and removal of dead or straggly branches will encourage healthy growth and keep the display looking trim. In summer a layer of pebbles, moss, or tree bark over any exposed soil in the pot will help prevent evaporation and weeds. Clean off any algae on the outside of the pots with a nailbrush and soapy water.

What to grow

Whether you grow plants singly or mix them is a matter of individual taste. A single specimen bay or clipped box will look formal and out of place in rustic surroundings, but a large, bushy fuchsia, underplanted with annuals could look wonderful in the same surroundings.

Mixed planting tends to create a pleasantly informal effect; traditional mixtures are fuchsias with petunias and trailing lobelia; pelargoniums with silver-leaved artemisia and alyssum. If you mix plants in one container, make sure they have the same feeding, watering, and exposure needs. For example, ferns, impatiens, and ivy will all enjoy the same shady spot.

►**All herbs and flowers**
Blend herbs with flowers in your container garden. The pale mauve flowers of rosemary blend well with the reds of snapdragons, the pinks and whites of the zonal pelargonium and the silvery leaves of the trailing Helichrysum *in the neighboring pots.*

---

tip

Turn to the sun
If your pots are in partial shade, you will need to turn them every now and then to stop them from growing lopsidedly toward the brighter-lit areas.

► **Framed to perfection**
A rather ordinary window can be transformed by lots and lots of pots—both free-standing and hanging—of pink and red zonal and ivy-leaf pelargoniums, which provide months of color and interest.

HANGING BASKETS

Inexpensive, easy to plant and look after, giving a mass of colorful flowers and greenery for months on end, traditional hanging baskets provide, in miniature, all the beauty of an old-fashioned country garden at the height of summer.

For an instantly eye-catching focal point, few things beat a hanging basket in full bloom. Whatever your garden's size, even if you have no garden at all, there's room for at least one hanging basket, and probably more. Hang them on one or both sides of a window or door; on porches or porch columns; on trellis arches, pergolas, or along a high boundary wall. A sheltered, sunny, or semi-shaded spot is best, away from passing traffic, but easy to reach for watering. Remember to allow space for plant growth, which can be surprisingly quick and substantial!

Choosing a hanging basket

There are many different kinds of container used as hanging baskets. The traditional favorite is a wire basket, which has the advantage of permitting you to insert plants through the sides, thus concealing the basket itself. This kind must be lined with some soft material to prevent soil and moisture from falling out. The same goes for baskets made of wooden slats. A plastic pot with a saucer attached will retain water but usually needs to be painted a neutral color to make it less conspicuous. Clay hanging pots are more attractive than plastic ones, but heavier, requiring extra-strong hangers. Some hanging pots and baskets have a flat side, for placing against a wall.

Unusual options include wooden buckets, wire salad shakers, even china chamber pots, hung with macramé!

▼ *Mixed charm*
Pink and red, mixed ivy-leaf geraniums find a happy home in this hanging basket set against a sunny wall in the garden.

Choosing plants

Any small-rooted, compact plant tolerant of container growing can be used, but graceful, arching, or trailing plants are ideal. The effect should be lush, so use filler plants, such as lobelia, to weave together feature plants, such as fuchsia, and upright plants, such as French marigold.

In a sunny spot, mix and match annual petunias, sweet alyssum, lobelias, and nasturtiums; and tender perennial zonal and ivy-leaf pelargoniums, wax and tuberous-rooted begonias, trailing verbenas, dusty miller (*Senecio cineraria*) and *Helichrysum petiolatum*.

In light shade, mix and match trailing fuchsias and lobelias, impatiens, star-of-Bethlehem (*Campanula isophylla*), nasturtiums, begonias, and dark-green or variegated ivy. Unusual options for shade include ferns, golden-leaved creeping Jenny, and spider plants.

Through the year Summer displays often remain colorful until the first fall frost, but you can use hanging baskets in winter and spring, too. Ivy on its own or as filler provides permanent interest, and comes in silver-, gold-, and red-variegated forms, as well as all-green. In winter, add winter-flowering heather, dwarf evergreen eunymous, or, in mild areas, dwarf cyclamen. In spring, add pansies, polyanthus, or crocus.

Caring for hanging baskets

Hanging baskets dry out quickly, so water regularly, once or even twice a day in hot weather. For high-level baskets, a self-locking pulley that can be raised and lowered is a good idea. Mist the plants in the evenings in prolonged heat waves. Feed with diluted liquid fertilizer every two weeks in spring and summer, and remove faded blooms to extend the flowering period and keep the display attractive.

▲ A study in contrasts
The restrained elegance of blue, white, and magenta trailing lobelia contrasts with the mix of fuchsias, ivy-leaf pelargoniums, lobelias, variegated ivy, impatiens, and spider plants in nearby baskets.

▼ Multiple impact
A single hanging basket can be lovely; two of them, at the peak of their flowering, as shown here, can be stunning.

PLANTING A HANGING BASKET

Materials
Wire basket, 15in (38cm) across
Black plastic sheeting
Damp **sphagnum moss** and damp **peat-based potting mixture**
1 trailing **fuchsia**
3 ivy-leaf **pelargoniums**
4 **petunias**
12 trailing **lobelias**
Large **flowerpot** or **bucket** to work on

1 Preparing the basket Place the basket on an empty flowerpot or bucket. Line it completely with ½in (1.5cm) thick moss. Cut the plastic roughly to fit, pierce a few holes for drainage, and loosely line the moss. Don't worry if it sticks up a little above the rim.

2 Adding the potting mix Fill one-third of the basket with potting mix. Just above the mixture, make 5 evenly spaced slits in the plastic with a sharp knife or pointed scissors. Working from the outside in, insert the roots of 5 lobelias, pushing them firmly into the soil.

▲ **Perfect partnership**
Deep blue trailing lobelias and red and pink fuchsias form a lush, dense globe of flowers and foliage. Dwarf annual China asters planted in the top of the basket are a charming finishing touch.

tip

Supporting the baskets
Buy strong metal wall brackets, with the bracket arm longer than the basket radius, so that the basket hangs freely. Use screws and anchors to fix. Always test a fixing before hanging a basket!

3 Planting the basket Fill two-thirds of the basket with potting mix. Make 8 slits and insert lobelias and petunias, alternating them and staggering them as shown.

4 Completing the basket Add potting mixture to within 1in (2.5cm) of the rim. Plant the fuchsia in the center, alternating 3 pelargoniums and 3 lobelias around it. Firm the soil and trim the plastic if necessary. Water thoroughly with a fine spray, then hang.

▲ Fiery and bright
Golden-yellow and flame-red annual nasturtiums create an eye-catching display, set against their own variegated foliage and variegated ivy. Though happy in sun, they are also ideal for light shade.

tip

Easy-to-use-liners
Line a wire or wrought-iron basket with a brown, pre-formed liner, made of compressed coconut fiber. This helps the soil to retain moisture.

▲ The more, the merrier
A garden in miniature, with lobelias, alyssum, ageratum, snapdragons, wax begonias, impatiens, fuchsias, and pelargoniums.

▼ A matching pair
Baskets of favorite English summer annuals: impatiens, petunias, French marigolds, lobelias, and Nemesia strumosa.

GLORIOUS WINDOW BOXES

For people without a garden, a window box provides a means of looking at a profusion of garden plants. If you do have a garden, it can provide a link between the outside and the interior of your home.

The best approach to planting window boxes is to plan a scheme that incorporates some evergreen plants, such as ivies and dwarf conifers, which will provide winter interest as well as green background. To these you can add a spring/summer collection of flowering plants. The types best suited to growing in a window box vary from season to season: the usual requirements are that they produce plenty of flowers in your chosen colors over a long period and that they have attractive foliage and relatively small roots. Just one window box can present many different opportunities for the plant enthusiast.

▲ *Cheerful flowering* A brightly burgeoning window box is a glorious sight. Be generous with a boxed display of seasonal flowers. A fuchsia provides the central focal point for this abundant display. On either side are ranged zonal pelargoniums in white and shades of pink. Lobelia and trailing pelargoniums cascade over the front, the pelargoniums adding interest with their ivy-shaped leaves.

See page 68 for a planting guide.

Containers

Window boxes can be bought in different materials and many shapes and sizes. Wooden, plastic, or terracotta boxes are available at most garden centers in a range of colors and finishes. Small boxes can look a bit lonely in the middle of a ledge, so choose a box that will fit snugly into the available space. Many modern houses don't have wide window sills; in this case there are ways of fixing the window box safely to the wall below the window (see page 68).

Window boxes should be at least 6in (15cm) from front to back, and 8–10in (20–25cm) deep, so they can contain enough soil to prevent the plants from drying out too quickly and to accommodate the root systems. Check that your window box has drainage holes.

Care and maintenance

Watering Containers dry out quickly, so frequent watering is essential. Apply the water to the soil, not the flowers and foliage, preferably in the evening or the early morning. Give enough water to moisten the soil thoroughly, then leave until the soil is almost dry before watering again. Overwatering a box is as harmful as underwatering.

If the sill slopes, use wedges to prop the box level and so ease drainage. Think about how the box will drain; if necessary, a drip tray can be placed underneath to prevent water from running down a wall or spoiling the paintwork on the sill.

Feeding To encourage flowering, give a regular liquid feed every two weeks. Dilute the fertilizer according to the manufacturer's instructions.

With permanent window box plantings, scrape off the top 2–3in (5–7cm) of soil every spring and replace with fresh potting mixture.

Selecting plants

The range of plants suitable for window boxes goes far beyond the familiar geraniums, lobelias, and petunias, although these colorful plants are popular for good reasons. Always put quality before economy, and make sure that the plants you buy are clearly labeled so you know exactly what they are. Even when your stock comes through a network of gardening friends, be choosy about the plants you accept for your window boxes.

To help with the selection, here are the pros and cons of the main plant types suitable for window gardens.

Annuals win all the way for summer color. Planted in late spring, they will bloom until early fall.

Perennials will live for several years,

▼ *A dazzling summer display*
Tuberous begonias, nasturtiums, French marigolds, and trailing Helichrysum *brighten what would otherwise be a dull wall. In this case the view from within is not worth keeping clear, so the tall begonias can take a central pride of place in the window box.*

◀ A burst of spring
A clay box brimming with yellow and purple crocuses heralds the spring. They are planted more closely than they would have been in open ground.

▼ Lightness and color
A ledge-less sash window is enhanced by an elegantly arranged window box. Pink zonal and ivy-leaf pelargoniums with rose-pink impatiens are placed in the center, with tall variegated abutilons flanking them on either side. Behind, delicate white marguerites rise up, while trailing lobelia and ivy cascade over the front rim.

but then tend to overgrow their allotted space.

Biennials, such as forget-me-nots and wallflowers, are planted in fall for spring color and go well with spring bulbs. Hostas, violas, creeping Jenny (*Lysimachia*), and periwinkle all do well.

Bulbs can be used for underplanting; they force their way up through the other plants when the season suits them.

Evergreens Small evergreen shrubs such as skimmia, eunymous, dwarf conifers and boxwood are useful for providing a framework of foliage, and dwarf types can be left in the box for several seasons to provide year-round continuity. Many evergreen plants have attractive berries as well as foliage.

▼ Red, white, and blue
A simple combination of red zonal pelargoniums and trailing blue lobelia has a fresh and cheerful impact against the white window and wall. The color of the pelargoniums is matched by the bright paintwork on the revamped window box.

tip

Year-round interest
To get the most from your window box, use a few evergreen plants which will look interesting once the summer plants have ended.

Trailing plants. Ivies (especially yellow- and silver-variegated ones) are attractive year round; in mild climates, periwinkles and silvery *Helichrysum petiolatum* will survive the winter.

Shrubby plants. Dwarf conifers, boxwood, *Aucuba japonica*, lavender, and rosemary are good choices.

PLANTING GUIDE

Follow this planting guide to reproduce the
window box display pictured on page 65.

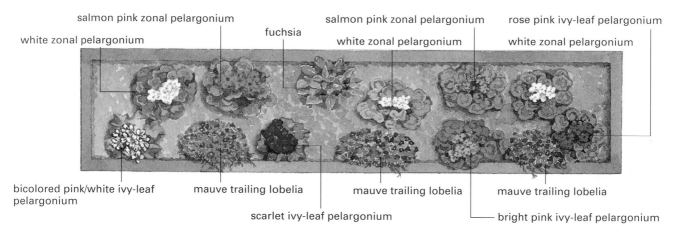

salmon pink zonal pelargonium

fuchsia

salmon pink zonal pelargonium

rose pink ivy-leaf pelargonium

white zonal pelargonium

white zonal pelargonium

white zonal pelargonium

bicolored pink/white ivy-leaf
pelargonium

mauve trailing lobelia

mauve trailing lobelia

mauve trailing lobelia

scarlet ivy-leaf pelargonium

bright pink ivy-leaf pelargonium

PLANTING UP

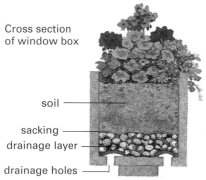

Cross section
of window box

soil

sacking

drainage layer

drainage holes

1 Put a 2in (5cm) layer of clay
pebbles or broken flowerpots in
the box over the drainage holes to
act as a drainage layer. Then cover
this layer with a sheet of sacking or
burlap, or a thin foam or sponge mat
to prevent the soil from washing
down. Fill the box to within 2in
(5cm) of the rim with a loam-based
potting mixture, as this retains
moisture well during warm weather.
If the box has to be as light as
possible, use a peat-based potting
mixture instead, although it will
need more frequent watering. Avoid
garden soil, as it may harbor pests,
diseases, and weed seeds.

2 Before planting up, position your
selection of plants according to
the illustration on the surface of the
prepared window box to get an idea
of how they will look. Put in the tall
fuchsia first, followed by the zonal
pelargoniums. Then insert the
trailing plants: ivy-leaf pelargonium
first and then the lobelia. Space
them more closely than you would if
planting in the open ground; the
relatively crowded arrangement
provides lots of color and interest
and the foliage should keep the
roots moist.

3 When planting is finished, fill in
the box with more potting
mixture to bring the surface to
within about 1in (2.5cm) of the rim.
Firm in the plants with your
fingertips and water them
thoroughly. Deadhead all plants
regularly, and clear away fallen
leaves and other debris.

SECURING THE BOX

A planted-up window box is
heavy, and on a high ledge it
needs to be properly secured for
safety.

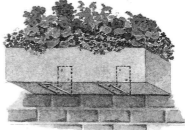

**Where the box rests on a
windowsill,** try putting a screw
eye into each end of the box,
with corresponding long-arm
hooks screwed into the window
frame. On a lower ledge, security
may be a problem; so as a
deterrent to thieves, use strong
wire instead of hooks.

When there is no ledge at all, or
an extremely narrow ledge, use
wall brackets to secure the box to
the wall. A pair of brackets will
support most boxes, but an
unusually heavy one may need
one or two more. If your box is
made of plastic, secure the
brackets with nuts and bolts
through the drainage holes.

If the brackets are exposed, use
concealed brackets or choose
ornamental wrought-iron
brackets, which are an
attractive alternative to the
ordinary L-shaped ones.

HERBS IN CONTAINERS

It's part of the magic of herbs that they will grow anywhere and in almost anything. The most popular herbs happily live in free-draining containers of all shapes and sizes—flowerpots, old sinks and troughs, urns, tubs, window boxes, hanging baskets, and half barrels.

Depending on size, the containers can be positioned outside in gardens, on balconies and patios, or on windowsills. Indeed, some herbs—unruly mint is the most obvious example—practically cry out for potting, because otherwise they'll overrun the garden.

▲ Lush greens
A group of culinary and medicinal herbs—feverfew, parsley, flowering chives and thyme, thrive in green glazed pots. Behind are sage, rue, and fennel—herbs that are as nice to look at as they are to use.

Choosing containers

Flexibility is a key factor when it comes to choosing containers for herbs. Traditionally, herbs were grown near the kitchen door, but you may wish to move your herbs around so as to catch the changing direction of sunlight, to bring them indoors for a spell, or simply to vary the decorative effect of a display. In this event, remember that large terracotta pots are harder to move than plastic ones.

Apart from their maneuverability, plastic pots also have the advantage of being cheap and easy to clean. Clay or terracotta pots tend to be more expensive, although no one would deny their rustic charm.

All containers need good drainage holes with a layer of gravel in the bottom as a precaution against waterlogging. Remember that soil in clay pots dries out more quickly than that in plastic pots, so frequent watering is required during dry spells. Indeed, it is a good idea to soak new clay pots in water for a couple of days before planting anything in them.

Starting a potted herb garden

Many herbs can be grown from seed, but some are difficult to raise successfully. It is much less trouble to start with healthy, well-formed plants from a good garden center.

The growing medium When transferring your herbs from the small pots they were bought in to your own containers, remember that it is not a good idea to use ordinary garden soil as the growing medium. This is likely to be full of weed seeds and perhaps other problems. Far better to purchase from a garden center some suitable potting mixture. Choose one that is made of sterilized loam, peat, sand, and fertilizer. Soilless, peat-based mixtures can also be used. Although they are lighter in weight, and therefore easy to handle, these mixtures have the disadvantage of running out of nutrients and moisture more quickly.

Feeding Newly potted herbs will not require fertilizer for at least a month because of the nutrients already present in the soil. After that time they will benefit from a weak liquid feed every two weeks in spring and summer, while they are being regularly harvested. Never feed herbs during winter, and beware of overdosing: read the label and follow the fertilizer manufacturer's instructions carefully.

▶ *Earthy tones*
This ornate terracotta urn, set against a brick wall, is home to bay and golden marjoram, flanked by silvery lavender cotton and Helichrysum.

◄ Good neighbors
Potted herbs are healthy in each other's company. Grouped together, they form a humid microclimate in which the individual plants thrive.

Scented steps
Rosemary and, behind it, lavender in flower, are both highly aromatic, woody herbs that do exceptionally well as potted plants.

▲ High-rise herbs
This unusual strawberry pot makes the ideal container for a collection of the most commonly used culinary herbs.

Watering Potted plants are vulnerable to drying out, especially in sunny weather, when the soil should be checked regularly. Basil, with its large soft leaves, needs frequent watering, while "woodier" herbs such as thyme and rosemary are less demanding. In general, herbs respond better to a regular soaking when their soil is dry than they do to an over-fussy regime of frequent slight waterings. If in doubt about a plant's moisture requirements, err on the side of dryness. On the whole, herbs are survivors.

Picking herbs

As a general rule, herbs should be picked little and often. Never take more than a quarter of the leaves from a herb at one cutting. A drastically harvested plant is a permanently weakened one.

Fragile-leaved herbs such as basil and tarragon keep a healthy bushy shape if the growing tip is removed or pinched out, and then the side leaves are picked. Although mint responds similarly, it's better to cut an entire stem, because then the plant responds with more succulent growth. With rosemary, thyme, sage, and winter savory, you can let the plant's appearance rule your picking strategy.

tip

Changing containers
When the roots of a herb are coming through the bottom of a pot, it's time to graduate to a larger container. The best time for potting on is spring, rather than the summer growing season or winter, when the plant is dormant and there are no new roots growing to anchor it in the soil. Tap-rooted herbs, such as parsley and dill, do well in deep pots.

Unusual herb containers

There are other less usual containers for a herbal garden. Attractive old ceramic sinks and wooden barrels can be receptacles for your favorite herbs.

If you are filling a hanging basket, whether you wish to plant a single herb or a group of them, choose a wire basket and line it first with wetted sphagnum moss, then with black plastic that has been punctured with drainage holes. Half fill the basket with potting mixture. Begin planting with a shrubby, bushy herb, such as rosemary, in the middle, and place low-growing herbs around this. Insert hanging or trailing herbs to cover the rim of the basket. Thyme, sage, or marjoram will trail attractively over the edge.

Parsley-only hanging baskets are popular, but these must not be suspended in full sun. On the other hand, basil in a basket loves the sun. Since a herbal basket needs regular watering, it's best not to hang it where the drips will fall on anything precious.

▶ **Window box**
Access is important when siting your potted herbs, both for care and for harvesting. A box on the kitchen sill is the answer. A selection of the most popular culinary herbs can be grown in a window box. Avoid mint, however, which will rapidly take over unless it is contained—in a pot or a piece of thick plastic cut to size —within the box.

▲ **Herbal wheel**
Set into the ground, this old cart wheel is a ready-made miniature garden, the different sections providing separate homes for individual plants. Popular cooking herbs, including several thyme varieties, are good neighbors for traditional therapeutic herbs like wild pansy (heartsease) and saxifrage.

◀ **Herbal hanging basket**
This basket is a happy home for a variety of decorative culinary herbs. Hang it near the kitchen door for easy access.

INDOOR GARDENS

In the middle of winter, when many garden plants are dormant—or even buried under a blanket of snow—you can still enjoy gardening inside the house, in a sunroom or sun porch. Such rooms are wonderfully adaptable to different lifestyles and different tastes in gardening. You can simply cultivate a few houseplants, give shelter to tender perennials, or create your own tropical paradise. In England, where they are called conservatories, these rooms are often constructed mainly of glass, so that they resemble a greenhouse, and are designed to serve as a visual link between house and garden.

Before choosing your plants, decide on the space you have available for them; whether the room is to be jungle-like or simply furnished with just a few plants. Also decide on the amount of time and energy you want to spend on them. Even expensive plants, if neglected, can quickly become eyesores.

▲ *Spring charm*
In the warmth and shelter of this elegant sunroom, tender buddleia, pelargoniums, calla lilies, and bougainvillea produce early blooms.

Practical factors

Minimum winter temperature is the main decisive factor in choosing plants. If you use the sunroom as living space all year round, then a winter temperature of 65–70°F (18–20°C) is ideal for tropical plants, such as *Stephanotis floribunda*, but unsuitable for those that need a winter rest period, such as cacti, pelargoniums, and ivy.

At the other end of the scale, an unheated sunroom benefits from solar gain and latent heat from the adjacent house but is still vulnerable to frost and unsuitable for tender plants. Some English conservatories are kept cool but frost-free over winter, at a temperature of 45–50°F (7–10°C), which saves on heating costs while still allowing a good range of plants to be grown.

▲ Variegated charm
Variegated pineapple plant and spider plant are combined with schefflera, begonia and calla lilies, for a cool, elegant effect.

For some plants, ironically, bright sunlight can be too much of a good thing. Ferns and other thin-leaved plants need shade, especially in summer. This can be provided by blinds, proprietary shading paint on the windows, or screen, or you could simply move the plants to a shady part of the garden in summer.

Plants' cultivation needs range from minimal, as with aspidistra, to challenging, as with staghorn fern, which needs special feeding and constant high humidity—incompatible with a carpeted sunroom floor. Most plants are sold with a basic care label, but if in doubt, ask before buying. Plants' rate of growth and ultimate size also vary enormously, from quick-growing, large trees, shrubs, or climbers, ideal for open-soil borders in a greenhouse, down to slow-growing cacti, which spend their whole lives in the same small pot. Again, if in doubt, ask.

Flowers or foliage plants

Flowers are universally appealing and add bright color, seasonal charm, and sometimes fragrance, to a sunroom. Their display, however, is short-lived, compared to foliage, which remains attractive half the year, if deciduous, or all year round, if evergreen. Foliage also provides a cool setting for flowers, which, in unrelieved mass, can look gaudy or overbearing.

Luckily, many flowering indoor plants, such as wax plant and clivia,

have foliage as attractive as their flowers; and many tropical foliage plants, such as coleus and croton, have leaves as colorful as any flower. Then, too, all green, or green-and-white, foliage schemes, can look highly sophisticated and restful, especially in summer.

Short-lived or permanent plants

Some houseplants, such as poinsettia, cineraria, chrysanthemum and coleus, can theoretically be kept year after year but are usually discarded when their flowers finish. Others, such as jasmine, oleander, and weeping fig, are long-lived and permanent fixtures. Including both types of plants ensures quick, inexpensive, seasonal color in a permanent framework, so that the room never looks bare. When buying repeat-flowering plants, get advice to find out how easy it will be to get the plants to flower again.

tip

Avoiding problems
Always inspect a newly bought plant for signs of pests or diseases before introducing it into your sunroom. Check the leaf undersides and young tip growth—both favorite spots for pests.

▲ *Garden glory*
In this cool conservatory, flowers including zonal pelargonium, fuchsia, dianthus, pansy, hydrangea, and French marigold thrive.

▼ *Permanent framework*
Rubber plants, aralia, ivy, and dracaena here provide an evergreen backdrop for daffodils.

▲ Study in green
Bamboos, palms, and other large-scale foliage plants create an elegant, jungle-like setting, with touches of color from the token flowers and the bowl of fruit.

▶ Showy foliage
In a warm sunroom you can grow all sorts of plants. Here you can see, from the top, sansevieria, calathea, Vriesea, *Dieffenbachia,* rhoicissus, *cordyline, croton, and bird's-nest fern.*

Decorative ideas

There is no right or wrong number of plants for a sun porch; it depends on your taste. You may love masses of plants or a sparse display.

You may simply want one or two small pot plants as accessories. Alternatively for a garden- or jungle-like effect, combine plants with a wide range of growth habits—upright palms, trailing ivies, ferns, climbing passion flowers, and so on—and let them intermingle. If you like color, add a few more flowering plants to this display.

The larger a plant, the more visual impact it will have. A single large specimen plant, such as a standard fuchsia or large camellia, can serve as the focal point for the room, around which smaller plants can be clustered.

You can be creative in your choice of colors for the plants' containers as well as for the plants themselves. Traditional terracotta pots are always appealing, but glazed china, stoneware, or bamboo cachepots can help emphasize a decorative theme.

3
A GALLERY OF COUNTRY PLANTS

PANSIES, VIOLAS, AND VIOLETS

With their appealing faces, pansies are among the most popular flowers for adding color to a garden. They make a charming display in beds, borders, and containers from mid-April to early summer. Although most die out in the summer heat, some will flower again in fall, if they are cut back and their roots kept moist. A few varieties flower in winter.

Technically short-lived perennials, pansies are usually grown as hardy or half-hardy annuals and are discarded after flowering. They grow up to 6–10in (15–25cm) tall, and 9–12in (20–30cm) across. Their flat, five-petaled, rounded flowers come in a huge range of clear and subtle colors, including white, yellow, orange, scarlet, blue, brown, and purple, many with contrasting blotches, veins, or eyes.

Closely related to pansies, and truly perennial, are violas, which grow to 2–6in (5–15cm) in height and 12–14in (30–35cm) across. They look like small pansies and come in a similar color range, but flower later into the summer.

Violets are perennial relatives of pansies. They have small, nodding, spurred flowers with narrow petals, in the white-blue-violet color range, and grow up to 3–6in (7.5–15cm) in height, and 6–16in (15–40cm) across. Violas and violets can be used as permanent

▲ Colorful palette
With their wide range of colors and color combinations, pansies can complement many garden schemes.

edging for beds, borders, and rock gardens. Many make excellent ground cover, especially under trees and shrubs.

Choosing pansies and violets
Pansies have the showiest flowers but require annual replacement. If they are planted in bedding schemes, they will need other seasonal plants to follow them. Violas and violets are less spectacular but are more natural-looking, and violets live longer. Consider the

flowering season; for spring and early summer blooms, the choice is wide; for fall and winter flowers, less so.

Color choice depends on personal taste and the garden's existing scheme, but with formal bedding, consider the color of the other components before planting. The darker the pansy, the less visible it will be, unless offset by silver or yellow foliage.

For fragrance, select sweet violets, *Viola odorata* hybrids. For low-maintenance ground cover, choose tough types, such as *V. cornuta* or *V. labradorica*, that are naturally carpeting and self-rooting.

Decorative ideas

Grouping plants Pansies look best grouped, whether in clumps of five or more tucked among shrubs and perennials or in blocks, rows, or circles in bedding. Violas and violets also look good in clumps or large, spreading drifts. The occasional self-seeded plant can be charming, simply growing between paving stones or mingling with other plants.

Formal or informal Pansies, with their relatively large flowers and compact, uniform, small leaves, are best for formal bedding, while for informal, wild, or woodland schemes, violas, with relatively modest flowers, clump-forming or spreading growth habits, and generous, often attractive, foliage, are ideal.

Choosing color schemes Single-color schemes tend to look more restful than multicolored ones, which have a bright, "carnival" feeling. For a cool effect, combine white, blue, mauve, or violet pansies with white or blue hyacinths or with cool-toned clematis. For a sunny, bright show, combine yellow or orange pansies with yellow or orange wallflowers and tulips. For a charming, pastel trio, combine pale pink shrub roses, lady's mantle, and pale blue pansies or violets.

Plant adjacent clumps of the violet-colored horned violet, *V. cornuta*, and "Alba," its white form. The resultant seedlings display an appealingly subtle variation in flower color.

Mixing plants Use pansies as dense "ground cover" for bedding tulips in spring and for formal rose beds in early summer. *V. labradorica*, "Purpurea," with its purple-tinged leaves and purple flowers, is excellent with pale blue striped squills (*Pushkinia scilloides*) or with golden-foliaged shrubs, such as the golden forms of elder, mock orange, or *Cornus*. Underplant the gray-leaved *Senecio cineraria*, variegated evergreen eunymous, or the creeping broom (*Cytisus kewensis*), with purple-horned violets, so they can climb and wander through the branches. Combine rue, gray-leaved *Hosta sieboldiana,* and white violets. Underplant a hedge with sweet violets and primroses. Combine pansies, miniature daffodils and dwarf topiary box for a spring display in a window box.

◄ Uniform choice
Block planting of a single pansy variety, such as "Arkwright Admiration," is effective.

▼ Attractive infill
Massed Viola cornuta *and its white form, "Alba," make a ribbon of soft color in a shrubbery.*

Popular types
Violas
The horned violet (*V. cornuta*) has evergreen leaves and long-stemmed, dark violet-blue blooms. There are white, light blue, and lilac named forms.

The Canada violet (*V. canadensis*) has white flowers tinged with purple at the edges, which appear in late spring.

Viola hybrids have slightly fragrant flowers, in many single and bicolor named forms, including the yellow and deep violet "Admiration," the claret-red "Rubin," and the purple-blue "Jersey Gem."

Violets
"Purpurea" (*V. labradorica*) has purple-tinged, evergreen leaves and small mauve flowers.

The garden violet (*V. odorata*) spreads by underground stems and has fragrant, deep violet flowers and hairy, evergreen leaves. Hybrids are available in white, pale and deep blue, violet, and pink and as double-flowered Parma violets.

The bird's-foot violet (*Viola pedata*), has lobed leaves and flat mauve flowers.

Pansies
The wild pansy or **heartsease** (*V. tricolor*) has small purple and yellow flowers in spring and early summer.

▲ *Spring medley*
Pansies, English daisies (Bellis perennis)*, spotted dead nettle, and grape hyacinths create a seasonal vignette.*

Buying and caring for pansies and violets

Buy plants in flats in spring for immediate planting; or buy and plant them in the fall (zone 7 and south) for early spring flowers. Choose sturdy, compact plants with healthy foliage. Violas and violets can be bought year-round in some areas. Buy fresh seed in fall or late winter.

Site in fertile, moist, but well-drained soil. Full sun or partial shade will promote lavish blooming; afternoon shade will prolong the flowering period in the south. Add well-rotted organic matter before planting pansies and violets. In pots, use a loam-based potting mixture.

Sow seeds in fall in a coldframe; or grow seedlings in a greenhouse, under lights, from winter, later placing them in a coldframe to harden off before planting outside.

Plant 6–8in (15–23cm) apart, firming them in well.

Care: Water until established, and deadhead regularly. Pansies kept outside during the winter should be mulched with straw or pine needles.

tip

Keeping cut violets fresh
Cut violets can absorb an enormous amount of water, so recut the stems and totally submerge them in cold water for several minutes, then arrange.

Garden pansies (*V. wittrockiana*) and hybrids are sold as mixtures, in color series, and as single-color varieties. Spring-flowering forms include "Azure Blue," "Springtime Porcelain Blue," "Black Prince," "Love Duet," with creamy-white, pink-centered blooms, "Flame Princess," with cream to yellow flowers and deep red blotch, the "Majestic Giants" and "Imperial" hybrids, and the solid-colored "Crystal Bowl" hybrids. Autumn- and winter-flowering varieties (zone 9) include "Beaconsfield," with dark and light blue flowers, and the mixed-color "Floral Dance" hybrids.

◀ Compact color
Pansies, which come in a range of bright and cheerful colors grow in self-contained clusters. Here they are shown bursting out exuberantly from a strawberry pot.

▶ Sweet sensation
Viola odorata, the perennial garden violet, forms a cascading carpet on these garden steps. The plant is particularly useful for areas where there is little soil.

▼ Color coordinates
A wonderful way to achieve a coordinated scheme is to use various shades of violets. Here the violets have been grown in a compact space, an old lead trough.

IRIS

With their delicate, yet elegant flowers, handsome foliage, and tough natures, irises make perfect garden plants, and they can be grown to enhance perennial or mixed borders, wild gardens, ornamental pools, or rock gardens.

In fact, irises are very versatile; depending on the species, they can thrive in dry or wet conditions, sun or shade, and acid or alkaline soils. Some make excellent, weed-smothering ground cover, others are good for gentle forcing in cool greenhouses, and many are ideal for cut-flower displays.

Irises have been collected and cultivated for centuries. There are hundreds of species with innumerable hybrids. They range from dwarfs growing 4in (10cm) high, to towering giants 4ft (1.2m) or more high. Because iris stems are sturdy, staking is rarely necessary. Flowers generally consist of three outer petals, or falls; three inner petals, or standards; and three narrow, petal-like arms.

"Iris" comes from the Greek word for rainbow, and the colors range from white through almost every shade to near black. Many irises also have attractive markings or veins, or are bicolored. Some are scented, have showy berries or even variegated leaves. Summer is the main season, but some cultivars flower in the spring and then again in early fall—in the South, even later.

Choosing irises
The size, color, and form of the flowers are important, especially in relation to where the plant will be set in the garden, but you should also consider the time of year, and the reliability and duration of flowering. Height, spread, and vigor of the plant should match the allotted space and position in the garden. Many irises will flower only briefly, so consider the appearance of the foliage; some are evergreen while others are deciduous. If you want low-maintenance ground

cover, choose those, such as *Iris sibirica*, that form dense clumps and happily tolerate semi-shade.

Irises vary enormously in cultivation needs, so it is best to choose a species that relates well to your garden's soil type, moisture content, aspect, and exposure. Most irises, once planted, can be left undisturbed for years on end, though a few, such as *I. X germanica* hybrids, need regular lifting, dividing, and replanting. Specialist bulb catalogs and nurseries offer a wider choice than garden centers, but ordering is best done well in advance, as you'll find many types are very popular.

▼ *A fine walkway*
Bearded irises make a colorful formal border to this unusual garden path, which leads to a porch. Bearded irises are very hardy plants which should be planted in neutral soil. They come in almost all colors and color combinations; here purple and yellow irises are predominant.

Decorative ideas

Formal or informal Densely planted, geometric beds of single-color, tall bearded irises will look impressively formal, especially if they are set into a lawn. On a smaller scale, try edging a straight garden path with single-color, bearded irises, to give a similar effect. Loose, irregular clumps of irises can enhance the informal quality of a woodland garden.

Mixing irises Irises look best planted in good-sized groups of single types, though adjacent drifts intermingling at the edges can be stunning. Try to plan these drifts so that one starts to flower as another finishes, so as to extend the display period. Devoting whole beds or borders to different types of irises, botanical-garden style, is much less effective than growing them in mixed planting, with a range of other plants, where their flowers and foliage contrast with the other subjects. They are particularly useful for adding color, when needed, to an early or late-flowering border.

Color schemes There are irises to complement or contrast with virtually any garden's color scheme. Bicolored irises or those with contrasting markings can set the color scheme for adjacent planting. Blue and yellow irises, for example, make good neighbors for such spring and early summer flowers as Canterbury bells, primulas, clematis, and *Campanula rotundifolia*. Deep, rich iris colors and soft smoky ones are less noticeable in the garden than the bold, clear, bright hues, but the softer-colored irises are especially lovely for indoor cut-flower displays or if grown in a raised bed surrounding a patio.

Plant partners Irises and old-fashioned roses, lupins, clematis, or peonies are traditional partnerships. Contrast pink roses or peonies with blue or mauve irises; complement buff-colored roses with apricot or orange irises; or blue, lavender, or wine-red clematis with matching irises, planted at the base.

Interplanting Grow *Iris reticulata*, snowdrops, and winter aconites for a low-level display. Combine yellow *I. pseudacorus* with *Euphorbia wulfenii* or *Artemisia absinthium*, for a summer show. In a dry, narrow bed at the base of a south-facing wall (zone 7 and south), combine *I. unguicularis* with one of your favorite evergreens for winter color. In waterside schemes, it is an idea to combine *I. sibirica* or *I. ensata* with hostas, candelabra primulas, ferns, and astilbes. Surround brightly colored Dutch or Spanish irises with gray-leaved *Senecio cineraria*.

Popular types of iris

Iris fall into four main groups; the first three groups are rhizomatous-rooted, while the last group is not.

Bearded irises have ruffled flowers, several per stem, with a hairy "beard" on the lower petals and gray-green, semi-evergreen leaves, which fall in fan-like sprays. They slip into three categories: dwarf, intermediate, and tall bearded iris hybrids. Bearded irises come in many colors and can also be bicolored. They all thrive in neutral, well-drained soil, and most bearded irises like a sunny sheltered site.

Popular tall bearded iris varieties are *I. pallida* "Argenteovariegata" and "Aureovariegata" which have lavender, bearded flowers and silver- and gold-variegated leaves respectively.

Beardless irises have smooth lower petals and are mainly bicolored, with several flowers per stem and long, narrow, mostly evergreen leaves. There are several popular varieties in this group.

I. ensata, or Japanese iris, also known as *I. kaempferi,* has clusters of single or double velvety, sumptuous flowers with broad falls. It should be positioned in a sunny area, but also likes moist soil, so it should be watered regularly. *I. sibirica,* with profuse blue

◀ **Easy-going choice**
Iris sibirica, *a beardless variety, thrives in rich, moist soil and puts on a fine show in the summer season, in appropriate beds or borders.*

▼ **Classy display**
Tall bearded irises are a popular choice for summer displays. Here, a white iris with purple-tinged petals basks in the sun. Note the beard on the lower petals.

▲ **Spanish charm**
These appealing Spanish Iris X xiphium *hybrids are moderately hardy Mediterranean varieties. They are smaller and later-flowering than the Dutch iris, but are equally good for indoor cut-flower displays.*

▼ **Wedgwood blue**
The Dutch Iris cultivar "Wedgwood" is a popular bulbous iris which blooms in late spring. It is an ideal plant for mixed borders and works well with yellow. Try planting "Wedgwood" iris with primulas and campanulas.

or white flowers, likes cool, rich, moist soil and a partially shaded site.

The California group of hybrids are also beardless and have dainty blue, purple, yellow, white, or red flowers on branching stems. *I. unguicularis*, another beardless hybrid, has rich lilac lavender flowers. It resents root disturbance.

I. foetidissima has small purple flowers, followed, in winter, by showy scarlet berries. *I. graminea* has dense tufts of narrow, glossy leaves and reddish purple and blue, richly scented blooms. **Crested irises** (*Iris cristata*) have much paler flowers with a showy, fringed crest on the lower petals, and evergreen, sword-shaped leaves.

A favorite variety is *I. tectorum* with lilac, white, and light purple crested flowers. Try to site this iris in an area of the garden that has dry, well-drained soil and light shade.
Bulbous irises grow from bulbs, not rhizomes, and have elegant, slender-petaled blooms.

A popular variety is *I. reticulata*, with tubular leaves and elegant, rather bright, blue, white, or purple flowers growing from fibrous-covered bulbs. *I. xiphium* hybrids are bulbous and are divided into English, Dutch, and Spanish types. All have reed-like leaves and slender-petaled flowers.

▶ Pretty patterns
In Britain's mild climate, the netted iris (Iris reticulata "Katharine Hodgkin") flowers from fall to midwinter, brightening up many a dormant garden. In North America I. reticulata blooms in early spring.

┌─tip─────────────

Bearded irises
Bearded irises should be lifted after flowering, every 2–3 years. Cut the leaves back by half, and divide the rhizomes into leafy, rooted sections. Discard the old central sections. Dust cut surfaces with fungicide. Replant the rhizomes facing the same direction, to receive sunshine.

◀ Winter color
Iris foetidissima is grown, in Europe, for these bright red seeds, which add color during the winter. The name is derived from the pungent smell of the leaves, when crushed.

Buying and caring for irises
Buy plump, dormant bulbs in fall, avoiding any shriveled or moldy ones. You can buy rhizomatous iris all year round, though the choice is best in fall and spring.
Site and soil should match the particular variety's needs.
Plant firmly as soon as possible after buying. Leave the tops of bearded iris rhizomes exposed, but plant beardless irises deeply. Plant crested irises just below the soil surface and bulbous irises 2–3in (5–7.5cm) deep.
Care: Water until established, and keep surrounding soil free of weeds. Divide clump-forming types immediately after flowering, as necessary. Cut back deciduous foliage in late fall.

CHEERFUL CHRYSANTHEMUMS

Whether grown in a greenhouse or, in the case of hardy perennial species, in the garden, chrysanthemums offer a wonderful splash of glowing color.

Chrysanthemums owe their popularity to their enormous diversity of size and color. Garden chrysanthemums are the simplest type, producing fresh and innocent daisy-like flowers, which can be single, semi-double, or double in form. They are often snow-white with a yellow center, but can also range through cream, yellow, orange, red, and rich russet to pink and mauve. Many annual forms are multicolored, with rings of bold colors on the petals.

Some garden chrysanthemums are hardy herbaceous perennials, while others are half-hardy perennials. You can also find hardy or half-hardy annuals. Plants range in height from 6in (15cm) for dwarf feverfew (*Chrysanthemum parthenium*) to 6ft (1.8m) or more for the giant daisy (*C. serotinum*).

Apart from the garden chrysanthemums, there is another huge category known as greenhouse chrysanthemums, which bear more exotic-looking, symmetrical blooms in a huge range of rich and subtle colors. There are two main sorts—large or medium types which are dis-budded so that they bear one very big bloom per stem, and spray types which produce spray heads of smaller flowers.

Greenhouse, or florist's, mums are among the most popular cut flowers. If you have a greenhouse, you will find that these plants amply repay the extra care required for their cultivation. If not, choose hardy species, which also

▲ Frilly "daisies"
Chrysanthemum maximum, *the Shasta daisy, is a traditional favorite in informal gardens. It can grow up to 3ft (90cm), and its tousled, white daisy-like flower heads appear in mid- to late summer.*

offer excellent flowers for cutting.

Perennial chrysanthemums for cutting were traditionally grown in rows in the vegetable garden, but they fit beautifully into perennial or mixed borders, and dwarf forms, as well as the much loved, old-fashioned, semi-hardy marguerites, are ideal for window box and patio planting. Free-flowering, bushy annual types can also be grown in borders, while dwarf annual forms make charming edging plants.

Choosing garden chrysanthemums

Decide whether you want annuals, which need replacing from seed every year, or perennials, which are longer-lived. If you choose perennials, determine whether you want the fully hardy types, which thrive for years with a minimum of care, or the hybrid greenhouse types, which require special cultivation under glass or, in mild climates, in a sheltered garden.

Most chrysanthemums have drab leaves and modest growth-habits, so flowers are the main attraction. Consider color, form, and size to complement nearby planting—also your interior color schemes, if you intend to cut them for flower arrangements.

Using garden chrysanthemums

Formal or **informal** French marguerites grown in containers as standards create a formal effect, especially when used in pairs, on either side of a front door. By its nature, dwarf chrysanthemum edging is also formal.

Mixing chrysanthemums Medium-sized and tall chrysanthemums benefit visually from contrasting foreground planting which hides their dull stems and leaves. In a border, chrysanthemums are usually most effective as large, informal clumps or drifts of one type; entire beds of a single type lack interest.

Partners for chrysanthemums

The early hybrids look good with the feathery foliage of bronze fennel or *Artemisia absinthium* "Lambrook Silver." Combine autumn-flowering giant daisy types with the blue spires of

▲ **Pink against mauve**
The double pink blooms of the French marguerite "Vancouver" stand out gaily against the soft mauve-and-white flowers on the lofty spires of Acanthus spinosus, *or spiny bear's breeches. Both perennials will flower freely through the summer.*

▶ **Annual color**
Chrysanthemum carinatum *is a half-hardy annual which grows rapidly from seed each year. Full grown, it ranges in height from 12–24in (30–60cm). The cheerful daisy-like flowers display rich purple centers and vividly banded petals, contributing a profusion of rich, bold colors to a thriving border.*

aconites. For an old-fashioned show in the garden, combine pyrethrums with lupins, lavender, catmint, and bearded iris.

White marguerites or Shasta daisies look lovely with white-variegated hostas. In a window box, try combining white marguerites with dwarf, white-variegated ivy and white petunias. Yellow marguerites (*Chrysanthemum frutescens*) can be planted with golden-variegated lemon balm or mint for a wonderfully bright display.

Popular varieties

Chrysanthemum carinatum is a half-hardy annual, with purple-centered, mostly single flowers. Seed strains include the dwarf "Court Jesters," the yellow and white "Northern Star," and the richly colored double "Double Mixed."

Chrysanthemum coccineum, the pyrethrum or painted daisy, is a perennial, hardy in mild climates, with single or double white, pink, salmon, scarlet, or crimson flowers, according to variety.

Chrysanthemum coronarium is a hardy annual, with white or yellow flowers, as a semi-double in "Flore Plenum" and a dwarf or semi-double in "Golden Gem."

Chrysanthemum frutescens (syn. *Argyranthemum frutescens*), the white or French marguerite or Paris daisy, has single or double white, yellow, or pink flowers, according to variety. Being tender, it is normally grown in a greenhouse.

Chrysanthemum leucanthemum, the oxeye daisy or moon daisy, is a hardy perennial, with white, yellow-centered daisy-like flowers. It is ideal for meadow gardens.

Chrysanthemum maximum, or Shasta daisy, is a perennial (also known as *C. X superbum)* with white, single, double, or frilled flowers, which blooms in summer.

Chrysanthemum parthenium, or feverfew, is a hardy, self-seeding perennial, often grown as a half-hardy annual, for bedding out. The flowers are mostly single or double white, or yellow in "Golden Ball." "Aureum" is grown for its golden-yellow, aromatic foliage.

Chrysanthemum serotinum, the giant daisy, is a hardy perennial that produces white flowers on long stems in summer.

Chrysanthemum x morifolium hybrids are hardy perennials. They include literally thousands of cultivars, some bred for the florist industry but many for the garden. The best garden types are early-flowering spray, pompon, and reflexed types with swept-back petals. Favorite cultivars include "Redcoat," with its glowing scarlet blooms borne in thick profusion; "Anastasia," with little pink button blooms; and the brown button form, "Dr. Tom Parr."

tip

Cutting chyrsanthemums
The day before the blooms are to be cut for indoor display, give the plants a good watering. Cut them with hand pruners the next morning while the stems still contain a lot of moisture. Strip the leaves from the bottom half of the stem before arranging. Re-cut stems every 2–3 days.

▲ *Golden choice*
A classic greenhouse chrysanthemum, "Golden Julie Anne" is an intermediate decorative form which can be grown outdoors in a mild climate. Half a dozen of these beautiful blooms will fill up a vase in a flurry of golden petals.

▼ *Pretty pompons*
"Purple Fairie" is an early-flowering, pompon variety of hybrid chrysanthemum. The clusters of spherical blooms consist of tightly packed, tubular petals in shocking cerise pink.

▲ Sunshine yellow
A raised container filled with the annual Chrysanthemum multicaule *creates a sunny focal point.*

▶ Formal effect
French marguerites, with their quick, semi-woody growth, are easily trained to form standards or half-standards. When grown in terracotta pots, they can also be moved around.

tip

Potted "mums"
If the ground is not frozen, plant potted chrysanthemums outside after they have finished flowering indoors. In mild areas, they will grow taller than before and should bloom the following year.

Buying and growing chrysanthemums
Buy fresh seed in autumn or winter; young, pot-grown hardy perennials in spring or fall; half-hardy types in pots during March and April.
Site chrysanthemums in a sunny, sheltered spot.
Soil should be well-drained and fertile.
Plant hardy types in fall or spring, and half-hardy types after the last frost, in well-dug and enriched soil.
Care: Keep plants well-watered in dry weather. Pinch out growing tips of annuals and spray-types to promote bushy growth. For large blooms, pinch out all side buds, leaving just the largest flower bud at the tip of the stem. Deadhead to encourage further flowering. Support tall types with twiggy sticks. Move delicate types to overwinter under glass.
Propagate hardy perennials from division and half-hardy types from cuttings in spring.

COLORFUL AZALEAS

Azaleas are brilliantly colored and free-flowering, popular shrubs. They are easy to grow in the right conditions, which include a lime-free, acid soil. They range from carpeting ground cover less than 8in (20cm) high to massive shrubs, which grow to 12ft (3.5m) or more high and across.

Their deeply lobed trumpet- or funnel-shaped flowers appear singly or as clusters from mid-spring to midsummer, according to type, and can be so profuse they completely hide the foliage.

All azaleas are now classed as rhododendrons, but the common name "azalea" is still widely used. There are basically two types of azalea, both of which have relatively small leaves.

Deciduous azaleas have flowers that range mainly from white to yellow, orange, and flame red, and are frequently fragrant. Their foliage often takes on brilliant color in the fall.

Evergreen, or Japanese, azaleas are technically semi-evergreen, since the leaves produced in spring drop in the fall, and only those produced in summer remain over winter.

Flowers are scentless, and colors range from tints of red with a hint of blue to clear pink, rose-pink, crimson, or magenta.

▲ **Semi-wild and wonderful**
Pink and flame-red Japanese azaleas, backed by somber green rhododendrons, surround a Japanese maple and set this part of the garden ablaze with color.

▲ Oriental pair
The elegant vertical growth and cool green of the bamboo Fargesia murielae complements the hot pink of Japanese azaleas in flower.

► Autumn glory
The leaves of the Ghent azalea hybrid "Emile" take on brilliant hues before falling in autumn. They would make an ideal backdrop for dahlias.

Choosing azaleas

Besides considering the ultimate height and spread of azaleas, think about the plant's flowering time and your garden's existing color scheme. Be careful of clashes, not only among groups of azaleas, such as yellowy pinks and bluey pinks, but between azaleas and other brightly colored spring flowers, such as forsythia and laburnum.

Variations on a single theme, such as tints of creamy white and yellow or tints of pale and deep rose, are usually harmonious in the garden.

In less than perfect conditions, choose deciduous azaleas or—in the South—Kurume hybrids. They will grow even in full sun, if they are well watered.

Popular azalea types

Most azaleas sold at garden centers are named hybrids of complex parentage. Knowing the group of hybrids to which your plant belongs will help you to assess its suitability for your garden.

Deciduous azaleas: The **Knap Hill** and **Exbury** hybrids are hardy and grow to 6–8ft (1.8–2.4m) high, with good spring and autumn leaf color. Their bright, sometimes scented, flowers are trumpet shaped. The plants come into flower in late spring.

Ghent hybrids grow to 6–12ft (1.8–3.5m) high and are very hardy and trouble free. Their small, scented, long-tubed flowers are ideal for informal planting and flower arranging. They flower in late spring and will also give good autumn leaf colors.

Molle hybrids—also known as Kosteranum hybrids—are mostly hardy plants. Their clusters of large, scentless, mainly yellow, salmon, or orange flowers bloom on leafless branches. They grow to 4–8ft (1.2–2.4m) high. Flowers can be seen from mid- to late spring and are vulnerable to frost, but plants give lovely leaf colors.

Occidental hybrids grow to 6–8ft (1.8–2.4m) in height, with fragrant, pastel-colored flowers which appear in spring.

Evergreen and semi-evergreen azaleas:

Kurume hybrids are moderately hardy and form dense, dwarf mounds, 2–4ft (60–120cm) high, of small leaves and flowers, which appear in mid- to late spring.

Gable hybrids are semi-evergreen or, in some cases, deciduous; but they are very hardy. They grow to a height of 3–6ft (90–180cm), and most flower in early to mid-spring.

Glen Dale hybrids have huge single or double flowers, up to 4in (10cm) across, on plants which grow 2–4ft (60–120cm) high. Though hardy, they prefer warm summers. Flowers appear in late spring

Kaempferi and Malvatica Vuykiana hybrids are semi-evergreen or deciduous, hardy and vigorous, with profuse, wide-mouthed, intensely colored flowers. Maximum heights are 2–5ft (60–150cm) and flowers appear in mid- to late spring.

Indicum hybrids are tender and usually grown as large-flowered pot plants, forced for winter flowering. Some forms survive outdoors in zones 8–10. Plants can grow up to 2ft (60cm) in height.

▲ Clear pink enchantment
"Flinomayo" is a very popular Kurume azalea hybrid which, originated in the Emperor's Garden in Tokyo. It is an evergreen plant and is phlox pink in color.

▼ A riot of color
Yellow, orange, pink, and flame are combined in this stunning display of deciduous azalea hybrids, which have been set against a woodland background.

▶ **Boxed in**
An evergreen azalea shares its home with variegated eunymous, ivy and Helichrysum, *for year-round interest.*

Buying and caring for azaleas
The choice is widest from fall through spring; go for pot-grown plants with a well-balanced, compact framework.
Buying plants in flower helps prevent disappointment later.
Site Free-draining, humus-rich, lime-free acid soil is ideal, and a sheltered, semi-shaded spot. In pots, use special, lime-free potting mixture.
Plant very early in spring or in late summer, when growth has ceased. In dry soil, plant deep and leave a shallow depression for water to collect on the surface. In wet soil, plant slightly high, forming a mound. Add slow-release fertilizer plus leaf mold, well-rotted compost or commercial potting mixture to the hole, and mulch the soil afterward.
Care: Water well during the first season, until established. In areas with limy water, use rainwater for azaleas growing in pots. In spring, lightly prune spindly young plants to make them compact; straggly older plants can be cut back hard. Mulch and deadhead annually.

Decorative ideas
Massing azaleas Drifts of azaleas make excellent ground cover, especially under light-foliaged trees, such as birch; or fill a shady border with them, such as along the shady side of your house. Underplant them with *Liriope muscari*, to provide autumn contrast.
Collector's garden On cool, acid soil you could create a stunning collection of azaleas, or azaleas with ivy and dwarf spring bulbs, such as grape hyacinth, to fill sheltered window boxes. Large tubs and beer barrel halves can contain a color-coordinated group of azaleas; or use them as ground cover, at the base of a formally clipped bay tree planted in square Versailles tubs.

Rock garden azaleas Plant a dwarf carpeting azalea at the top of a shady rock garden, to provide tumbling sheets of color in spring.
Partners Flowering dogwoods and azaleas, Japanese maples and azaleas, are natural partners, since they like similar conditions. One or two azaleas can enliven a bed of dwarf conifers. Azaleas also go well with other members of the *Ericaceae* family, such as mountain laurel, leucothoë and gaultheria.

▼ **Perfect partners**
A pink-flowered deciduous azalea and drift of bluebells team up to create a delightful garden vignette.

SUNNY DAHLIAS

Dahlias are among the most eye-catching flowers, with their vivid blooms which last from midsummer until autumn. The plants range from 10in to 5ft (25–150cm) high; the flowers, from dainty pompons to dinner-plate size, in all colors but blue, and in many bicolors. Charming and unsophisticated, dahlias are ideal for adding a country-garden touch anywhere. Dahlias can be divided roughly into two categories: tall dahlias, which are often used in borders, and low ones (also called dwarfs or miniatures) which are used for bedding. They are further divided into more precise groups based on the kind of flower they produce.

All grow from tuberous roots, which are normally lifted a few days after the first frost and stored for the winter.

▲ Decorative dahlias
A mass of richly hued pink dahlias provides a welcome splash of color above a rustic picket fence.

Although tubers can usually survive the winter in zones 8–10, they should be lifted and the clumps divided in order to produce the best blooms. Some small bedding dahlias can be grown from seed.

Choosing dahlias

When you are choosing dahlias, think about the planting space available in your garden, your favorite color scheme, and whether having flowers for cutting is a priority. Check the packets for the size of bloom: huge blooms can be spectacular but they need support and can look unreal; smaller blooms look more natural in a garden setting and tend to be self-supporting.

Pastel colors create a soft, old-fashioned look; bright, clear hues give a more cheerful, carnival-like feel; and subtle, smoky tones can look sensational against colorful fall foliage.

Decorative ideas

Grouping dahlias Dahlias have most impact when planted in groups, against contrasting backgrounds. For example, if you have a dark green hedge, plant bright, pastel, or white dahlias; conversely, a white wall looks good with dark, rich, or bright hues.

Formal or informal Plant dahlias informally, in clumps of three, five, or seven plants, or in formal rows to make bold blocks of color.

Choosing color schemes Single-colored groups of dahlias tend to be more restful on the eye than mixed colors. Silvery shrubs, such as *Senecio cineraria*, rosemary, or lavender cotton, help cool down "hot" dahlia colors, and are equally effective with pale tints. Combine silver foliage, pink dahlias, and pink and white cosmos for a soft, misty effect.

For rich autumnal hues, combine red or orange dahlias, red-hot pokers, marigolds, calendulas, and nasturtiums.

For a study in white and green, grow dahlias, perennial sweet peas, snapdragons, and hollyhocks, all in white.

For dramatic impact, grow scarlet dahlias against green and gold variegated privet, weigela, or dogwood. For sizzling color, grow clumps of mixed dahlias and mixed zinnias.

Mixing plants If you have long-stemmed flowers, such as mallow, hollyhocks, or gladioli, you can disguise their bare stems with medium-height dahlias.

Taller-growing types can fill gaps left by sweet Williams, forget-me-nots, and other late-spring flowers.

Interplant tall dahlia tubers among delphiniums, lupins, and foxgloves. Once these finish, cut away the faded flowers and let the dahlias take over.

▶ *Vivid color*
*Orange dahlias with the annual white mallow (*Lavatera trimestris*), which have been planted to hide the spent stems of montbretia behind.*

▶ **Vibrant tones**
A riot of autumn colors creates a bold display against an old blue frame house. The tall dahlias in this border mix well with chrysanthemums.

▶ **Contrasting flower shapes**
Colorful summer bedding plants in a cheerful and informally haphazard planting include multicolored dahlias, yellow zinnias, and dwarf sunflowers.

When to cut
Cut dahlias first thing in the morning before the sun has reached the flowers and while they are still full of sap. They can also be cut after the sun has set.

Popular dahlia types

Dahlias are classified according to the structure and size of the bloom. Unless you're showing, categories don't really matter, but they do give you an idea of what's available.

Single dahlias look like brightly colored daisies. Self-supporting, they are ideal for bedding, mixed borders, and cutting.

Anemone-flowered dahlias have flat outer petals and pincushion-like centers. Good for mixed borders, bedding, and cutting for flower arrangements.

Collerette dahlias, similar to anemone-flowered, are often bicolored, with an outer and inner ring of petals round a central disk. Especially good for cutting.

Water-lily-flowered dahlias bear flat, double flowers with no central disk; petals are relatively few, but wide and sometimes curve inward.

Decorative dahlias are double, with broad, flat, blunt-tipped petals. They range from small to enormous, and are good for cutting.

Ball and the smaller **pompon** dahlias are spherical, with inwardly curved petals. They are good for garden displays. Pompons are long-lasting when cut.

Cactus- and **semicactus** are double-flowered, with long, pointed, rolled petals. Ranging from small to huge, they are good for cutting.

A **"miscellaneous"** category includes various smaller groups such as liliput dahlias, whose small size adapts well to containers.

Bedding dahlias

Bedding dahlia seed strains offer a wide range of flower shapes and colors, usually on dwarf or compact plants. "Redskin" has red foliage; "Dwarf Dahl-Faced" has a branching habit; and "Early Bird" flowers early. Most are mixed colors. Single-color strains are ideal for formal bedding.

Storing dahlia tubers
Line a slatted wooden box with a thin layer of dry peat. Place the tubers on top of the peat and cover with more peat. Leave in a frost-free, dry area over winter. Check for mold occasionally and wipe clean.

▲ **Potted dahlias**
Dwarf dahlias grow particularly well in pots. In autumn, let the pot dry out and take the container indoors for the winter. Add water when you put the pot out again in late spring.

Buying and caring for dahlias

Tall dahlias are usually sold as dormant tubers labeled with the variety's name. Choose plump tubers, with no sign of disease or sprouting. When buying young **bedding dahlia** plants in pots or trays, choose compact plants with buds showing color.

Site: A sunny, sheltered spot is best, and deep, rich, moist but loam-based potting mixture.

Plant tubers 4in (10cm) deep in mid-spring, and bedding dahlias after the last frost.

Care: Water well in dry weather, stake tall-growing and top-heavy types, and deadhead regularly. Disbud, or remove side buds, to encourage single, large blooms. Lift tubers after the first hard frost, rub off any soil, cut the stems 1in (2.5cm) above the tubers, and store in a cool, frost-free spot.

◄ *Walled flowerbed*
A mixture of single pink bedding dahlias intermingle with perennial garden pansies in a raised walled bed.

▼*Borders of pink*
Single border dahlias are planted as an edging to provide a welcoming mass of color beside a pathway.

PRECIOUS SWEET PEAS

With their delicate petals, luscious colors, and ravishing scent, sweet peas are among the best-loved of all flowers. They require a little pampering, though. Disliking hot weather, most species will not survive the summer, except along the coasts of the Pacific Northwest and New England. Elsewhere, they can be grown successfully in a greenhouse. Apart from these annual sweet peas, there are a few perennial forms, which can be grown in the garden.

The plants range from 6in to 10ft (15cm–3m) high; many are climbers that cling by means of tendrils, but a few are non-climbing, bushy forms. The flowers, 1–2in (2.5–5cm) across and carried up to seven per stalk, range from white through pink, salmon, scarlet, crimson, lavender, purple, and blue—virtually every color imaginable. Some are bicolored or marbled in contrasting tints.

Choosing sweet peas

Your choice of sweet pea depends partly on your climate and partly on the amount of time you are willing to devote to them. Early-flowering annuals, grown in a greenhouse, will flower from October through January if sown the previous July. If you live in an area with cool summers, you can sow the seed indoors in February, harden off the seedlings in a cold frame, plant them out once the soil is workable, and enjoy their blooms throughout the summer. The

▲ **Best of both worlds**
"Leamington" a deep lavender-blue sweet pea, has large, strong-stemmed blooms. The flower also has an exceptionally sweet scent.

less-demanding perennial sweet pea can be grown from purchased plants, placed directly in the ground. All types except dwarf and bush varieties should be grown up a support of some kind.

Seeds come in mixed or single colors; choice depends on taste. For cutting, grow mixed colors; you can pick one color for a monochromatic display, or mix two or more colors. Some varieties are more fragrant than others.

Decorative ideas

Grouping Sow small patches of sweet peas in mixed borders, to provide carpets or pillars of color, according to height. If you want large, colorful blooms and heavy fragrance, grow a few plants of a strongly scented but modest-looking, old-fashioned variety, in among the large-flowered Spencer varieties.

Formal or informal support Bamboo poles, pea sticks, and plastic netting, can be used as supports, but you can also grow tall annual or perennial varieties up either side of an arch or pergola, to meet in the middle. For an informal effect, let sweet peas clamber naturally over early spring-flowering shrubs, such as *Choisya ternata*, whose show finishes just as the sweet peas start, or let them sprawl over sunny banks.

Color schemes Unlike some mixed-color garden flowers, mixed-color sweet peas have a natural harmony, and a single packet of seeds can provide all the color you wish. Pastel pinks, blues, and mauves are typical, and, in a garden, complement, or pleasantly contrast with roses, phlox, or clematis in a similar color range.

Mixing plants Mix low-growing forms with other hardy annuals such as corn-flower, larkspur, or evergreen candytuft, for an informal, old-fashioned effect. Grow a row of tall sweet peas along the back of a one-sided border, but make sure you have access, for care and cutting. For cooling color contrast, use lady's mantle, with its acid-green flowers, as edging to semi-dwarf sweet peas.

Popular sweet pea types

ANNUAL sweet peas are all forms of *Lathyrus odoratus*.

Dwarf and semi-dwarf varieties These mixed-color types grow from 6in to 3ft (15–90cm) high. The smallest, such as the "Cupid," are self-supporting and ideal for edging, pots, and window boxes. Semi-dwarf types need minimal support and make excellent flowering hedges. Varieties include "Patio," with wavy petals; "Bijou," an early flowering and heat-resistant plant; and "Soopersnoop," which is sprawling and tendrilless and has long-stemmed flowers, which are good for cutting.

Galaxy varieties These make robust, heat-resistant climbers. In addition to "Galaxy Mixed," single-color forms include "Scarlet Whizz," "Lavender Delight," and "Blue Argo."

Old-fashioned varieties These have heavily fragrant but small flowers on climbing stems. They are available as "Old Fashioned Mixed," the royal blue and violet "Fragrant Beauty," and the carmine and white "Painted Lady."

Spencer varieties The most popular sweet peas, these climbers have large flowers, some fragrant, ideal for cutting and showing. They come in mixed and single colors, including the lavender blue "Wisteria," the white "Swan Lake," the bicolored "Love Match," the creamy-white, sweetly scented "Hunter's Moon," and the rose-pink "Gypsy Rose."

PERENNIAL sweet peas are hardy herbaceous types. They include *Lathyrus latifolius*, with its gray-green leaves and unscented, pink flowers, rosy pink in "Rose Queen" and white in "White Pearl," and *L. grandiflorus*, with unwinged stems and large, distinctive, rose-pink and red flowers.

---

tip

Techniques for flowers
Sow singly in special, sweet pea "grow-tube" fiber pots. When the flowers are 8in (20cm) high, pinch out all weak shoots. Plant out and regularly tie in the main shoot, cut all tendrils from the leaf tips, and pinch out all side shoots. Remove all flower shoots with fewer than four buds, as they are generally weaker.

▲ Midsummer medley
A low-growing, multicolor sweet pea hedge forms a foreground to roses, lobelias, petunias, fuchsias, verbenas, and pansies, for a cheerful and vivid summer display.

▶ Shocking pair
The everlasting pea Lathyrus latifolius "Rose Queen" partners the orange-peel clematis, (C. orientalis) for a colorful, late-summer display on a wooden trellis.

◀ Distinctly different
A favorite old cottage-garden plant, the everlasting pea (L. grandiflorus) has exotic-looking, orchid-like blooms, in a stunning fuchsia-pink color with a maroon red keel.

▼ Flying the flag
"Red Ensign," a strong-growing, sweetly fragrant variety of sweet pea with rich scarlet blooms, is one of the many single-color, climbing forms available. These plants are happiest if they are attached to climbing frames in the garden.

▲ Traditional support
Twiggy hazel pea sticks provide discreet, natural-looking support for climbing types of sweet peas. If you want a less informal support, use bamboo poles, upright or tied together in a tepee.

▼ Old favorites
Fragrant, fragile, and colorful, annual sweet peas are among the most popular garden and florist's flowers. They are ideal flowers to pick if you like delicate blooms decorating the house.

tip

Cut flower life
Keep cut sweet peas out of drafts and well away from ripening fruit and vegetables and older flowers, all of which give off ethylene gas, which is harmful to the blooms.

CHARMING CAMPANULAS

Campanulas, also called bellflowers or harebells, include a huge range of old-fashioned herbaceous perennials, biennials, and alpine plants, popular mainly for their blue, single or double bell-, star-, or cup-shaped flowers.

Carried singly, in spikes or loose clusters, they provide a welcome, cool contrast to the hot pinks and reds of roses, peonies, phlox, and geraniums; and to the sharp yellows and oranges of lady's mantle and daylilies. In rock gardens, campanulas follow the first flush of spring color, overlapping aubretias and alyssums, to partner pinks, thrift, and saxifrages.

Most campanulas are easygoing, hardy deciduous perennials, which gradually form good-sized clumps. Some are biennial and a few are evergreen, tender, or a bit more challenging to grow. Many make ideal ground cover, in time creating stunning carpets, drifts, or vertical accents of color.

▲ Pink and white profusion
Massed pink and white Canterbury bells fill a border, backed by mixed-color foxgloves, including a few rich, deep pinks, for added depth, and peachy-pinks, for sharp contrast.

Choosing campanulas

Campanulas are usually blue in color, ranging from pale and milky to deep violet-blue, but there are also white, lavender, and soft-pink forms.

Sizes range from alpines that are only 2in (5cm) high, to huge species with flower spikes up to 6ft (1.8m) high; and from slow-growing, compact plants, for flower pots and trough gardens, to rampant colonizers needing firm control.

Most taller types, such as the milky bellflower, *Campanula lactiflora*, bloom once, in late spring to early summer; some low-growing types have a longer flowering period. For example, the Adriatic bellflower (*C. elatines* var. *garganica*) blooms continuously from late spring to early fall—a bonus in a small garden. The more familiar bluebell (*C. rotundifolia*) bears its deep blue or white flowers from late spring to late summer.

▼ **Golden leaves** *"Dickson's Gold," the yellow-leaved form of the Adriatic bellflower,* C. elatines var. garganica, *adds a sunny splash of color to a rock garden.*

Decorative ideas

Campanula foliage is unremarkable, and tall types look best with their lower stems hidden by plants such as shrubby cinquefoil, lady's mantle, *Senecio cineraria*, or hosta.

White and pale campanulas are effective in light shade or against dark backgrounds, such as ferns, laurustinus, or yew.

Dark campanulas show up best in bright settings, such as against a whitewashed wall or a yellow-leaved dogwood or philadelphus.

For an informal rose garden, plant clumps of campanulas, lady's mantle, and lilies among shrub roses.

In hanging baskets grow the tender, trailing star-of-Bethlehem (*C. isophylla*). In a large basket, combine it with trailing fuchsia.

Naturalize the bluebell (*C. rotundifolia*) in rough grass or the giant bellflower (*C. latifolia*) in a woodland garden.

Trough gardens are ideal for the dainty fairy thimble (*C. cochleariifolia*).

Back-of-border trio Combine magenta *Geranium psilostemon* with the pale blue bellflowers of *C. lactiflora* and dark blue aconite.

For edging beds and borders, try the Carpathian harebell (*C. carpatica*) spaced at 12in (30cm) intervals.

Sequential interest Lift border campanulas after they flower, and transplant them to a spare plot. Fill the space with *Lobelia cardinalis*, dahlias, cosmos, or chrysanthemums.

On the wall Scatter seeds of *C. elatines* var. *garganica*, *C. poscharskyana*, or *C. portenschlagiana* in the spaces between stones of an old stone wall, or in the cracks between paving slabs on a patio or terrace.

For formal impact, grow the steeple bellflower (*C. pyramidalis*), or Canterbury bells (*C. medium*) in large pots on a patio or on either side of a front door.

Brighten a shady corner with Japanese laurel (*Aucuba japonica*), placing low-growing *C. poscharskyana* and golden creeping Jenny (*Lysimachia nummularia* "Aurea") in front.

Fill a shady window box with ivy, dwarf campanula, such as *C. carpatica* or *C. elatines* var. *garganica*, and soapwort.

Popular campanula types

Garden centers usually display popular varieties in perennial and rock garden sections, with biennials featured in early fall, and star-of-Bethlehem in the houseplant section. Specialist alpine perennial nurseries carry unusual types.

Border perennials include *C. alliariifolia*, 2ft (60cm) high, with creamy-white flower spikes; the clustered bellflower (*C. glomerata*), 18in (45cm) high, with tight clusters of blue-purple flowers; and the peach-leaved bellflower (*C. persicifolia*), 3ft (90cm) high, with spikes of saucer-shaped blue or white flowers. For the back of the border, the milky bellflower (*C. lactiflora*), 5ft (1.5m) high, has sprays of blue, white, or pink blooms; and the giant bellflower (*C. latifolia*), has 6ft (1.8m) high spikes of tubular blue or white flowers.

Rock garden types include *C. arvatica*, 2in (5cm) high, with starry blue or white flowers; *C. carpatica*, 12in (30cm) high, with large, cup-shaped blue, white, or purple flowers; *C. cochleariifolia*, 6in (15cm) high, with thimble-shaped blue flowers; *C. elatines* var. *garganica*, 6in (15cm) high, with star-shaped blue flowers; and the invasive *C. portenschlagiana*, 6in (15cm) high, and *C. poscharskyana*, 12in (30cm) high, with flowers carried singly, and in spikes respectively. The harebell (*C. rotundifolia*), 6–12in (15–30cm) high, has blue, purple, or white bell-shaped blooms.

Biennials include Canterbury bell (*C. medium*), 1–3ft (30–90cm) high with cup- or cup-and-saucer-shaped blooms; and the rare chimney bell-flower (*C. pyramidalis*), 4ft (1.2m) high, a perennial grown as a biennial, for flowering in midsummer.

▶ Star-of-Bethlehem
Also known as the Italian bellflower, C. isophylla *is a tender perennial usually grown as a houseplant. In cool climates, it can be used as summer bedding—as shown here with lobelias and begonias.*

▼ Orchard extravaganza
An old apple tree forms the focal point for a drift of white and blue peach-leaf bellflowers, which are perennials, and a few self-sown foxgloves.

Buying and caring for campanulas

Buy containerized plants from early fall to mid-spring. Check the label for expected height and spread; ask garden center staff about the rate of growth, since strong-growing types may swamp weaker neighbors.

Site Most grow equally well in sun or light shade; tall-growing types need shelter.

Plant in any well drained, fertile garden soil, spacing 8–24in (20–60cm) apart.

Support Insert twiggy sticks or plant supports for tall types, when planting or when growth starts in spring. Don't wait until they need support, since it is then awkward to do.

Care: Water new plants until established. Deadhead after flowering, to conserve the plant's energy and, with *C. persicifolia*, to encourage a second flush in fall. Protect alpines from slugs and snails; some may also need protection from winter rain.

▲ *Free-flowering beauty*
The Carpathian harebell (C. carpatica), is non-invasive and easy to grow and forms clumps of showy, bell-shaped flowers in late spring and early summer. White, dark blue, violet, and late-flowering varieties are also available.

▶ *Perennial border blues*
Clustered bellflowers (C. glomerata) bold and rich blue, contrast with delicate pale pink flowers of London pride (Saxifrage x urbium) in early summer. When these finish, nearby sedums will provide replacement interest.

ELEGANT FUCHSIAS

With their graceful, pendent flowers, arching stems, and neat foliage, fuchsias are widely loved. They make superb greenhouse plants, and can also be grown outdoors in the garden during the summer. Some varieties are hardy in warm areas, such as the South and California.

They range in height from 6in–6ft (15cm–1.8m) or more, in mild climates. The flowers can be single, semi-double, or fully double, and carried singly, in pairs or clusters. Colors range from white and cream to pink, salmon, orange, scarlet, crimson, lilac, and violet. Many are bi-colored, and a few have variegated leaves.

Fuchsias can add country charm to a garden, growing in the open ground, against walls, or in pots or hanging baskets.

The few varieties of fuchsia that are hardy in the United States (zone 7 and south) include *Fuchsia magellanica* and some hybrids derived from it. These can, of course, be left in the ground permanently. Most fuchsias, however, are tender and must either be brought indoors and overwintered in a cool but frost-free spot or simply discarded.

Choosing fuchsias

Decide first whether you want a permanent or temporary feature: tender fuchsias need more care and attention.

Consider size, type of growth, and available space. Some plants are erect, others are floppy, standard-grown fuchsias put on a fine show in minimal space. Consider the color in relation to nearby plants. "Fuchsia" pink can be jarring next to yellow or orange; golden-leaved fuchsias can enliven a dull, shady bed. Small, single blooms are often more elegant and natural-looking than double types, which have more impact when they are seen from a distance. Some fuchsias flower sparsely; others so profusely that the foliage is hidden by the flowers.

▼ *Fuchsia profusion*
Three lavish fuchsias—"Lena," "Swingtime," and "Tennessee Waltz,"—make a colorful display against a wooden fence.

Decorative ideas

Focal point Group pot-grown fuchsias for an effective focal point on a patio, wide steps, or path. Use several different-sized pots of the same basic shape and material, such as terracotta. Include trailing, bushy, and upright or standard fuchsias, in harmonizing colors. Whole beds of fuchsias tend to be less successful, lacking sufficient contrast.

Formal or informal Repetition is the key to achieving formality with fuchsias; try pairs or rows of identical standards in white Versailles tubs or identical trailing fuchsias in hanging baskets. Otherwise, fuchsias have a natural informality which can be used to advantage, especially when they are used in mixed planting schemes.

Choosing color schemes

Most fuchsias fall within the pink-red-purple range, and can mix happily with these colors, or with blues and white. White fuchsias look cool and sophisticated, ideal for shady, all-white, or mainly foliage gardens.

Careful positioning A few fuchsias, such as "Orange Crush," "Orange Mirage," and "Nell Gwyn" (*sic*) have a definite yellow tinge, and need careful siting, well away from the pink-purple types, but with similarly colored roses, calendulas and French marigolds.

Mixing plants Combine fuchsias, ferns, and hostas in a moist, lightly shaded spot. In sun, combine fuchsias with the brilliant magenta rose campion (*Lychnis coronaria*) and summer hyacinths (*Galtonia candicans*).

Center spot Use a trailing fuchsia as the centerpiece of a hanging basket, with lobelia and ivy-leaf pelargoniums planted around the edges, or a row of dwarf or trailing fuchsias in a window box. Fuchsias also grow happily in terracotta pots, if you prefer to plant them in these.

Up a wall Against a warm, sunny wall, fuchsias may reach 6ft (1.6m) high or more. Fasten the stems back as they grow, and plant a toning, late-flowering clematis, or silvery *Senecio viravira* for company.

Border ideas Use tender fuchsias to follow sweet Williams, wallflowers, or Canterbury bells in a mixed border.

▲ **Crimson and rosy pink**
The tender, double "Prosperity" has thick, waxy, crimson sepals, pale rose petals, flushed and veined rosy red, and glossy green foliage.

▼ **Variation on a theme**
Tender fuchsias fill a hanging basket to overflowing, their graceful shapes echoed by a standard fuchsia in the shady garden beyond.

▲ Hale and hardy
The spreading, hardy Fuchsia magellanica "Versicolor" makes a striking addition to a border, and can be grown as hedging in mild areas.

▼ Pink and white charm
The tender "Hula Girl" has pink, backward-pointing sepals and densely packed white petals, reminiscent of a ballerina's skirt.

tip

Buying the best
Try to buy a plant in flower, so you know what you are getting; but don't automatically pick the one with the most flowers. It may have weak or unbalanced branches, or have exhausted itself in flowering.

Popular fuchsia types

Fuschias have a wide range of uses in the garden. The large hardy shrub types make excellent bush hedging plants or can be grown against a wall. The standards make marvelous ornamental plants in borders or containers, while the dwarf and trailing types are ideal choices for window boxes and hanging baskets.

Hardy fuchsias include *Fuchsia magellanica* varieties, such as "Alba," with bright green leaves and light pink flowers; and the vigorous "Riccartonii," with scarlet and purple flowers. Among the hybrid fuchsias that are hardy in warm zones are "Fanfare," with elongated, bright red flowers; "Royal Purple," with large purple and cerise, semi-double flowers; and "Mrs. Popple," with scarlet and purple single flowers.

Tender bedding fuchsias are shrubby or upright hybrids used in formal bedding, in mixed borders, and for container growing. There are dozens of named hybrids, but "Swingtime," with fully double white and red flowers, "Thalia," with reddish leaves and clusters of orange-red flowers, and "Tennessee Waltz," with double mauve and pink blooms, are all popular.

Trailing fuchsias have a naturally lax habit and are ideal for hanging baskets and window boxes. Tender hybrids include the single rose-pink and cerise "Display," the double red "Trailblazer," and the compact semi-double pale pink and purple "Lena."

Standard fuchsias are upright, quick-growing tender hybrids grown as a single stem, then pinched out to form a "mop-head" top. Half-standards have short stems; "tabletop" standards are even shorter. They are ideal for container growing and as pot plants in bedding schemes. Popular standard hybrids include the semi-double pink and white "Miss California," and the single red and purple "Mission Bells."

Dwarf fuchsias include the miniature "Tom Thumb," with small scarlet and mauve single flowers; "Lady Thumb," with semi-double white and pale carmine flowers; and the pale pink single "Gladys Miller."

Buying and caring for fuchsias

Buy containerized hardy fuchsias in early or mid-spring, and tender fuchsias after the last frost. Choose a well-balanced, strong branching system, true to type. Avoid any with unnaturally yellow or wilting leaves or whiteflies.

Site Choose a sheltered, sunny or lightly shaded site and ordinary, well-drained but moisture-retentive soil. Use loam-based potting mixture in pots, peat-based in hanging baskets.

Plant as soon as is convenient after buying. Plant firmly, so the surface of the potting mixture is level with the surrounding soil. Water well. Stake standard fuchsias in exposed positions.

Care: Water regularly and mist-spray in hot weather. Feed weekly during the growing season. Deadhead regularly, and remove any shoots that form on the main stems of standards. Move tender types under cover in fall and harden off, before moving out in late spring. Mulch hardy types in fall. In mid-spring, cut back all types by a quarter, and cut any dead wood back to ground level.

▲ White on white
"Ting-a-Ling," with its flared, bell-like petals, is perfect for an all-white or mixed-color scheme, where the normal range of fuchsia colors could clash with the other bedding plants.

▼ Golden leaves
"Golden Marinka" is a popular species of fuchsia, with wonderfully colored leaves. It, and the many other varieties of Fuchsia magellanica, *make excellent garden shrubs in mild climates; hardy fuchsias can also make spectacular hedges.*

tip

Overwintering tender fuchsias
Before the first autumn frost, move pots into a cold, but frost-free greenhouse or garage. Remove and discard any accompanying annuals, then water lightly. Water every 2–3 weeks from then on. Once temperatures drop, the leaves will fall. When signs of growth appear, cut back by a quarter, then increase watering.

STATELY DELPHINIUMS

Among the tallest and most impressive herbaceous perennials in the June border, delphiniums are universal favorites. Their vertical, often dazzling, flower spikes are equally at home in meadow gardens and formal perennial borders, and delphiniums are surprisingly adaptable plants, bringing country-fresh charm to the garden wherever you choose to plant them.

Delphiniums range from alpines, growing barely 6in (15cm) high, to magnificent giants, 8ft (2.4m) tall or more. Blue varieties, from milky pastel tints to deep, rich hues, are the most popular, but there are also white, creamy yellow, pink, mauve, and red forms. Some have contrasting central eyes, or "bees," of an inner ring of small petals. The cup-shaped, spurred, and sometimes hooded florets can be densely or loosely packed on the stem. The hardy annual delphinium, or larkspur (*Consolida* spp.), provides quick color in the garden and is found fresh in cut-flower displays and dried for winter arrangements.

Choosing delphiniums

Height is a prime factor, dictating whether the plant goes in the front, middle, or back of a border. Remember that the tall types are vulnerable to wind and generally need staking.

The typical, blue-to-white delphinium color range goes with virtually anything. If the surrounding scheme is pastel, you could emphasize it with pale blue delphiniums, or add lively contrast with dazzling, rich blue. In a richly colored border, pastel or white delphiniums add a restful note, or you could continue the theme, with intensely blue varieties.

Pale delphiniums are especially effective against a dark setting, such as a yew hedge; rich, deep blue types show up best against pale or white brick, stone, or rendered walls.

▶ **Dark-eyed beauty**
"Lillian Bassett" is a black-eyed, white-flowered D. elatum *hybrid. It is especially spectacular grown against a dark green hedge.*

◀ **Cottage-garden charm**
Delphiniums take their traditional, back-of-border positions in this profuse display of typical English cottage garden flowers, including columbines in variety, sweet Williams, lilies, and campanulas.

▼ **Outstanding pair**
Delphiniums and roses, especially old garden roses, make a natural partnership. The fresh green delphinium foliage conceals the lower stems of the rose bushes, and the roses provide contrast in color, form, and often fragrance—the only thing missing from delphiniums, which are otherwise perfect garden flowers.

Decorative ideas

Grouping delphiniums Their strongly vertical quality is most effective *en masse*, so plant groups of at least three of any one variety together. If planting more than one group, remember that each group has a strong visual pull, so site them with care, perhaps at either end of a bed, or opposite each other in adjacent beds.

Formal or informal For formal effects, rigid types with densely packed spikes are best. Planting groups symmetrically also creates formality—clumps of delphiniums on either side of a front gate, for example. Naturally branching types or those with loose, airy flower sprays have an informal, relaxed appeal.

Color schemes Rich blue delphiniums fronted by mustard-yellow *Achillea filipendula* "Gold Plate" or brilliant blue delphiniums, fronted by heleniums and edged with multicolored zinnias are guaranteed focal points.

For a trio in blue, front tall blue delphiniums with the blue peach leaf campanula (*C. persicifolia*) and edge with blue *Tradescantia x andersoniana*.

Pastel blues and pinks have a soft, peaceful quality: pale peonies, lupins, campanulas, and delphiniums, in variety, would make a charming garden picture. For an all-white scheme, combine white delphiniums, *Spiraea arguta* "The Bride," white-flowered clematis, and silvery-leaved artemisia.

Mixing plants For early season interest, plant tulips among clumps of delphiniums. After they have bloomed, the

tulips' fresh green foliage will provide a lovely setting for the delphiniums.

Back delphiniums with climbing roses, such as the creamy-white "Wedding Day," or grow clumps of delphiniums among shrub roses, such as the old-fashioned moss rose "Gloire de Mousseaux," or the modern shrub rose "Morden Blush."

Plant *Clematis recta*, with its delicate white flowers, to ramble over clumps of delphiniums. Frothy white seakale or baby's breath flowers also make a good setting for delphiniums.

Popular delphinium types

Consolida ambigua Rocket larkspur (also called *Delphinium ajacis*) is an annual, growing 1–3ft (30–90cm) tall, with branching stems of loosely packed blue, pink, violet, or white flowers. The hyacinth-flowered hybrids, with double blue, or white flowers, are popular.

Delphinium x belladonna The hybrids grow up to 3–5ft (90–150cm) high and have graceful, branching, slender stems bearing loose sprays of flowers. "Blue Bees" is light, bright blue, "Lamartine" deep blue, "Pink Sensation" clear pink.

Delphinium cardinale This moderately hardy species reaches 2–3ft (60–90cm) in height and has loose racemes of lustrous, scarlet flowers in summer. Rich, moist soil in full sun is best.

Consolida species. Larkspur, an annual growing up to 4ft (1.2m) high, is much branched, with densely packed flowers in white, pink, red, purple, or blue. "Giant Imperial Mixed" has double flowers on 4ft (1.2m) spikes; "Stock-floweret" is also double, 3ft (90cm) high. Single-color strains include "Blue Spire" and the carmine "Dazzler."

Delphinium x elatum These hybrids have sturdy stems, and can grow from 3 to 8ft (90cm–2.4m) tall, densely packed with flowers. Dwarf named forms include "Blue Heaven," double medium blue; "Royal Flush," pink with a white bee; "Blue Tit," indigo with a dark bee; and "Mighty Atom," deep lavender. Taller named forms include "Fenella," brilliant blue with a black bee; "Galahad," white; "Black Knight," dark blue with a black bee; "Blue Nile," medium blue, with a white bee; and "Strawberry Fair," dusky pink, with a white bee.

Delphinium grandiflorum These plants grow more than 2ft (60cm) tall, with branching spikes of violet-blue flowers, white in the form "Album." *D. grandiflorum* is a short-lived perennial, but is sometimes grown as a half-hardy annual for summer bedding.

Delphinium nudicaule This species is unusual in having spikes of orange-red, long-spurred flowers, which grow up to 2ft (60cm) high.

Delphinium tatsienense This is a gem for a rock garden and grows a mere 8in (20cm) tall in spikes of gentian-blue flowers. It is short-lived, but self-seeds freely.

▲ Bold and regal
Adjacent clumps of D. elatum hybrids, with their dense flower spikes in medium blue and intense, deeper blue, form a natural focal point in any bed or border.

◄ Carnival of color
Annual delphiniums, or larkspur, provide quick, inexpensive splashes of color, in mixed, as shown, or single-color seed strains.

Buying and caring for delphiniums

Buy container-grown perennial delphiniums from fall to mid-spring. Spring-bought plants should have plump shoots.

Larkspur seeds should be bought from late winter on; check the date on the seed envelope,to make sure it is fresh.

Site: Choose a sunny, sheltered site and deep, rich, moist but well-drained soil; larkspurs tolerate light shade. Dig over the ground, removing all weeds.

Sow larkspur in early fall, or early to mid-spring, where it is to flower. When large enough to handle, thin the growth to 10–16in (25–40cm) apart, according to type.

Plant perennial delphiniums 1–2ft (30–60cm) apart, according to type. Water after planting.

Care: Water in dry weather. Stake tall delphiniums; support tall larkspurs with twiggy sticks. Deadhead after flowering to encourage a second display in autumn. In late fall, cut all flower spikes back to ground level. Protect autumn-sown larkspur with cloches in winter. If slugs and snails are a problem, use slug pellets.

▲ Light and airy
"Blue Bees" displays the airy grace, branching habit, and loose flower racemes typical of the Belladonna range of hybrids.

◄ Connoisseur's choice
For a delphinium out of the ordinary, choose D. cardinale. Its scarlet, yellow-centered, bonnet-like blooms are carried in graceful, loose sprays.

tip

Smaller delphiniums
If you grow giant delphiniums but want smaller spikes for flower arranging, cut off the flowering shoot tip when it is 6in (15cm) tall. Several laterals will form, each a perfect spike in miniature.

POPPY DAYS

Informal and eye-catching, poppies light up the garden and countryside in late spring and summer. Though the gorgeous silky or crepe-papery, cup-shaped blooms look fragile, the plants themselves are generally tough and hardy, and once established they are usually self-sufficient.

They can be annual, biennial, or perennial, and range from alpines, 6in (15cm) high, to towering, back-of-the-border subjects, 4ft (1.2m) or more in height. Most have lobed or deeply cut, shiny, or hairy, leaves.

True poppies—those belonging to the genus *Papaven*—have single, semi-double, or fully double, ball-like blooms, some with fringed petals. Colors range from white through shades of yellow, pink, and orange to the traditional scarlet and magenta, often with black blotches or black centers.

The closely related Himalayan poppy has clear, sky-blue blooms. Individual poppy blooms are short-lived but profuse, and their distinctive bulbous, flat-topped seed pods are welcome additions to dried-flower displays.

▲ Oriental splendor
Among the most popular perennial border plants, oriental poppies are stunningly beautiful. The foliage dies down in midsummer, but cutting back hard after flowering encourages new growth and a second crop of flowers.

Choosing poppies

In addition to height and spread, consider the color scheme of nearby plants. Decide whether you want permanent or short-lived plants, but remember that some perennial poppies have deep, penetrating roots, difficult to get rid of once established, and most annual poppies self-seed.

Taller types with huge flowers need staking, especially on exposed sites. If you have a cool, shady garden, choose Welsh or Himalayan poppies, though the latter are short-lived and definitely a challenge to grow!

▶ Subtle and seductive
The soft-pink, maroon-blotched flowers of the opium poppy, growing among its unripe seed pods. Because this poppy is a source of the drug, its cultivation is illegal in many hot countries.

▲ Mixed border beauty
Orange poppies, old-gold achilleas, and russet-red pansies create an unusual early summer trio. Later, the achillea flowers and poppy seed heads can be picked and hung upside down to dry, for use in dried-flower arrangements.

▶ Hot and cold
The hot pink of these Shirley poppies is visually cooled by their white centers and rims. Seed strains of fully double Shirley poppies are also available.

Popular poppy types

Alpine poppy *(Papaven alpinum)* is a hardy, short-lived perennial, 6–10in (15–25cm) high, often grown as an annual. It has white, yellow, apricot, or pink flowers, up to 2in (5cm) across and grows all summer.

California poppy *(Eschscholzia californica)* is grown as an annual. It reaches a height of 16in (40cm) and has lacy leaves and satiny single or semi-double flowers. These poppies bloom in white, orange, yellow, red, orange, bronze, or pink—all summer long if sown in succession. They self-seed readily and in warm climates are often perennial.

Field poppy/Shirely poppy *(P. rhoeas)* is a hardy annual, up to 2ft (60cm) high. The original form, also known as Flanders or corn poppy, has crinkly-petaled, orange-red flowers with black blotches, in early summer. The cultivated Shirley poppy varieties are single or double, with white, pink, orange, or red, white-centered blooms.

Himalayan blue poppy *(Meconopsis betonicifolia)* is a short-lived but beautiful perennial, 3–5ft (90–150cm) tall. It needs moist, rich soil in cool shade. Its sky-blue, yellow-centered flowers appear in early summer. It dies after flowering if allowed to flower in the first year, and is best replaced from seed.

Iceland poppy *(P. nudicaule)*, also called arctic poppy, is a short-lived, very hardy perennial, up to 30in (75cm) tall, usually grown as a hardy biennial or half-hardy annual. It has rosettes of soft green leaves and crepe paper-like flowers, in white, yellow, pink, red, and pastel shades. Self-seeds readily.

Matilija poppy *(Romneya coulteri)* is an invasive, moderately hardy shrub, up to 6ft (1.8m) tall, with pinnate leaves and brilliant white, papery flowers with golden stamens during mid- to late summer. It needs light, well-drained soil and sun.

Opium poppy *(P. somniferum),* a hardy, self-seeding annual up to 30in (75cm) high, has large single or double, fringed, white, pink, red, or mauve flowers, with dark markings. Flowers in early summer and has huge seed heads.

Oriental poppy *(P. orientale)* is a sprawling but popular hardy perennial. It grows up to 4ft (1.2m) high, with deeply cut leaves and scarlet, white, pink, or deep red, single, semi-double or double flowers, up to 16in (40cm) across, some-times blotched. It flowers for a relatively brief period in late spring. Its roots are difficult to get rid of once established.

Welsh poppy *(Meconopsis cambrica)* is a hardy perennial, up to 18in (45cm) high, with ferny leaves and lemon yellow to orange flowers which last all summer long. Plant in sun or light shade. Single-flowered forms self-seed freely; double-flowered forms do not.

Decorative ideas

Formal or informal Poppies have a natural informality, especially if allowed to grow and seed at will, but oriental types can make an impressive contribution in formal perennial borders, and dwarf annuals make unusual formal edging.

Filling gaps Use annual poppies to follow spring-flowering bulbs and bedding plants. Partner oriental poppies with baby's breath, so that the frothy baby's breath hides the bare patch left when the poppy flowers and foliage die away in midsummer. Alternatively, plant asters or garden chrysanthemums in front of oriental poppies, to flower as the poppies finish.

Scatter seed of annual poppies, especially *P. rhoeas,* in a semi-wild garden, on a sunny bank, in rough grass or in cracks between paving slabs. When self-seeded poppy seedlings appear, don't automatically pull them out. Unless you have a very specific scheme in mind, leave the poppies to add bright spots of color and visually weave the planting scheme together.

Choosing color schemes Swathes or drifts of a single-color poppy are more restful to the eye than multicolor plantings, which have a livelier, more exuberant effect.

For early summer contrast, underplant pale mauve rhododendrons with Welsh poppies; or pale lavender irises with the shining pink oriental poppy "Raspberry Queen." Combine pink poppies with pink and blue columbines and pink lupins or delphiniums for an old-fashioned, English cottage-garden effect. In a white garden or bed, plant the stunning oriental poppy "Black and White" for its dazzling blooms.

▲ Compact and colorful
"Fireball" (P. orientale nanum plenum*) is a dwarf, free-flowering perennial, with scarlet-orange double flowers. Only 18in (45cm) high, it increases to large clumps.*

▼ In the pink
Scarlet is the traditional color for poppies, but for softer, pastel color schemes, there are pink, salmon, and white named varieties of oriental poppy.

Buying and caring for poppies

Buy pot-grown perennials in fall or spring. Save the label, in case of mislabeling. Seeds are available from garden centers and seed catalogs.

Site: Sandy, light, dryish soil and full sun are best for most poppies; Himalayan poppies need rich, cool soil and shade.

Plant perennials in fall or spring. Sow annuals in spring or fall (or in a greenhouse in cold climates), and biennials in early summer, where they are to flower, since they do not transplant easily.

Care: Stake oriental poppies; annuals are self-supporting. Cut back oriental poppies after flowering for a second, autumn crop of flowers. Lift, divide, and replant old perennial clumps in spring, or propagate from root cuttings. Deadhead to prevent self-seeding and prolong flowering.

tip

Picking poppies
To prevent poppies from drooping when cut, pick erect, nearly open buds in the evening, dip the stem tips briefly into boiling water, or sear with a flame, then place in deep, cold water overnight. Poppies exude a milky white or yellow sap which can irritate skin, so wash your hands after handling cut poppies.

Unusual poppies

A selection of unusual poppies has been featured on this page to give you the chance to choose a range of different poppies for your garden.

▲ *California sunshine*
California poppies thrive in poor, dry soil and hot sun. The species have yellow or orange blooms, but varieties come in a wide range of single or mixed-color seed strains, including the popular "art shades."

▼ *Blue beauty*
*The Himalayan poppy (*Meconopsis betonicifolia*), unlike other kinds of poppy, needs cool, humus-rich, lime-free, moist soil and light shade. Ideal for a sheltered woodland garden, it is best replaced regularly from seed.*

◄ *A sunny touch*
The cheerful, vivid yellow Welsh poppy is doubly valuable, since it flowers as profusely in light shade as in sun. Rampant self-seeders, Welsh poppies soon spread far and wide!

HARDY GERANIUMS

If you are looking for easy-to-manage plants, hardy geraniums, or cranesbills, may be the answer. They are attractive and give weed-proof ground cover all summer.

Larger geraniums are best suited in backs of borders, centers of island beds, and wild gardens. Medium-sized ones can be used to fill gaps between shrubs and other perennials in mixed borders, or act as "edge breakers," visually softening straight-edged paths.

Because geraniums are dense and quick-growing, they make ideal plants for ground cover. They also work out less expensive than other, slower-growing plants, such as bergenia and hosta.

Dwarf geraniums easily find a niche in rock and trough gardens; some thrive on stone walls or between paving slabs.

Most hardy geraniums are easy-going, clump-forming herbaceous perennials, with five-petaled, saucer-shaped flowers, 1–2in (2.5–5cm) across, and deeply cut or lobed leaves.

They are sometimes confused with tender pelargoniums. Though related, these plants differ in some respects.

Hardy geraniums have looser flower sprays than the tight, ball-like pelargonium clusters. Both have white, pink, lilac, or red flowers, but only hardy geraniums can be blue. Both also have the long, pointed seed cases, or carpels, that give geraniums their common name, cranesbill.

▼ **Bright cluster**
Brighten up a dull part of the garden with geraniums. Here Geranium psilostemon, *popular in Britain, provides a vivid splash of color.*

Choosing hardy geraniums

Geranium flowers range in color from white through pink, salmon, magenta, crimson, lavender, blue, violet, and near black. Most flowers are single, but a few are semi-double or double; some have attractive contrasting veins on the petals or centers.

Geraniums generally flower in early to midsummer, but some flower in late spring also. Leaves vary—some look solid. Others are lacy and delicate. Leaf colors also vary, ranging from gray to dark green, and can be matte or glossy.

Dwarf geraniums are semi-evergreen, but a few of the larger geraniums are evergreen. Some turn fiery colors before dying in autumn, others turn rich russet and remain over winter, until replaced by new spring growth.

Heights range from 4in (10cm) for the tiny *Geranium cinereum* to 4ft (120cm) for *G. psilostemon*.

Decide on the location first, then consider the height, form, flower, and foliage color and display season of adjacent plants.

Low-growing geraniums are especially effective with plants of contrasting, upright, or arching shapes, such as hostas, ferns, and Solomon's seal.

Decorative ideas

Old favorites Underplant yellow shrub roses with "Johnson's Blue." For old-fashioned edging, combine "Johnson's Blue," pale-pink *G. endressii,* and pale blue catmint.

To maximize the impact of the deep red *G. sanguineum*, grow it with silver and blue foliage, such as rue, and a selection of ornamental grasses, such as blue fescue.

Choosing color schemes Feature yellow and white geraniums in a late-spring display, with pale yellow daylilies, *Dicentra spectabilis* "Alba," *G. sylvaticum* "Album," and variegated foliage. Edge dark purple columbines and ornamental onions with the dusky white, purple-veined flowers of *G. renardii*.

For color later in the summer, edge hydrangeas with *G.* "Russell Pritchard" and the blue-centered flowers of the African daisy (*Osteospermum eklonis prostratum*).

For early spring interest, plant snowdrop, anemone, and crocus bulbs with *G. wallichianum* "Buxton's Blue."

◀ **A hint of pink**
Emphasize a favorite color against a background. This G. endressii "Wargrave pink" really stands out against Astilbe simplicifolia "Alba."

▲ **Small but special**
Geraniums are very adaptable plants and fit into many areas of the garden. Smaller plants and dwarf geraniums are great for filling any nooks and crannies. Here a purple G. cinereum finds a home of its own in the rock garden.

▶ **Color display**
Using mixtures of geraniums of similar shades, you can create stunning effects. Choose various shades of pink, and plant dwarf geraniums at the front and larger ones toward the back of the display.

▼ **Old favorites**
Geranium "Johnson's Blue" is a popular choice among many gardeners. To give your garden an old-fashioned atmosphere, use this plant along path edges. It's also an ideal choice for borders.

Popular geranium types

In garden centers, geraniums can usually be found in either the herbaceous perennial or the rock-garden section.

Tall types include *G. psilostemon*, 4x2ft (120x75cm), with black-centered magenta flowers and brilliant autumn leaf color.

Medium-sized types include *G. endressii*, 18x24in (45x60cm), with chalk-pink blooms; *G. endressii* "Wargrave Pink," 2x3ft (60x90cm), with salmon-pink flowers; the similar but double-flowered *G.* "Plena"; *G. macrorrhizum*, 1x2ft (30x60cm), and *G. sanguineum*, 12x18in (30x45cm), both with magenta flowers.

Low-growing types include *G. cinereum*, 4x10in (10x25cm), with gray, leaves and pink flowers, and *G. dalmaticum*, 6x24in (15x60cm), with light-pink flowers and glossy leaves.

▲ Rocky charm
Dwarf geraniums are ideal plants for rock gardens. A pale lilac geranium, G. renardii, *has been used in this rock garden. The plant's pale flowers contrast well with the moss on the rocks. Geraniums tend to spread, and if you want to keep them under control, the plants will need cutting back regularly.*

◄ Back to nature
Ferns are perfect to mix with this tall geranium, as they help to highlight the plant's color. This G. endressii's *salmon-pink flowers stand out well against the green background. This is a great way to show off a plant with a small flower, which might otherwise be lost, as they tend to blend into the background.*

▼ Going wild
Allowing geraniums to spread will give your garden that Old-World charm. Almost hidden among the plant's leaves is a stone seat. This peaceful look is achieved simply by allowing the geraniums to go back to the wild and spread naturally.

Choosing and care
Buy container-grown plants; from mid-autumn to mid-spring.
Site: Border types grow in sun or light shade, but *G. phaeum* prefers shade. Most rock garden types prefer sun. Tall-growing types need shelter from wind.
Plant from mid-autumn to mid-spring, in ordinary, well-drained soil, 6–24in (15–60cm) apart. Avoid over-rich soil, which leads to lush foliage and few flowers. Plant *G. cinereum* in spring.
Support tall types with twiggy sticks, bent over and inward at the top to make a "roof," before stems start to grow.
Water carefully until well established, then only in very dry weather. Cut back stems hard after flowering, to promote a second flush of flowers. Lift and replant every 3–5 years.

BRILLIANT BEGONIAS

Among the tender ornamental plants, begonias reign supreme for their beauty and versatility. They also have an accommodating ability to continue flowering for months on end.

In the United States, begonias are grown mainly as houseplants. Indoors, they thrive in gentle, filtered sunlight and in warm, but not hot, temperatures. Many do well under artificial light. Where summers are cool, some begonias can be taken out into the garden, where they make an impressive display in beds and borders and in containers such as window boxes and hanging baskets. The hardy begonia (*Begonia grandis*) can live outdoors all year round in zones 6–8.

There are over a thousand different species and varieties, from tiny cultivars a few inches high to huge, bamboo-like shrubs and climbers. The waxy, single, semi-double, or double flowers range from modest to spectacular and come in every color except blue and mauve. Leaves, likewise, range from tiny to huge and from modest to stunning, many being variegated or textured.

Cultivated begonias can be divided into five basic types. Tuberous-rooted types, popular for hanging baskets, are mostly deciduous and grown for their showy male blooms. Fibrous-rooted types, such as wax begonias, are evergreen and shrubby, and are grown

▲ **Splendid blooms**
Begonia "Midas" displays the sumptuous yellow, rosebud-like blooms typical of the tuberous-rooted varieties. In the background you can see stunning red and pink varieties of Begonia "Midas" too.

mainly for their flowers. Rhizomatous types, including rex begonias, are grown mostly for their evergreen foliage. Shrubby types are multi-stemmed, with evergreen leaves and single flowers, while cane-stemmed begonias or angel-wing types produce hanging clusters of showy pink or coral red flowers and glossy evergreen leaves on sturdy stems.

Choosing begonias

The color and shape of the begonia flowers and leaves are obviously significant, but it is also very important to match the plant's location to its ultimate size, too. Consider the plant's appearance in relation to nearby plants—especially if it is to be used in summer bedding schemes—or, if it is to be displayed indoors, with your decor.

Another crucial decision to make when choosing your begonias is whether you want a floral or foliage effect, or both, and whether you are prepared to overwinter or discard deciduous types when dormant. Most begonias bloom in spring and summer, but a few flower in winter. Some, such as wax begonias, are easy to grow; others are much more challenging. Wax and tuberous-rooted types are the most popular for outdoor use, but houseplant begonias are ideal for displaying on a patio from late spring until the first frosts.

Ways with begonias

Formal or informal Compact begonias used as bedding or edging tend to have formal overtones, while those with a loose or trailing habit convey informality, though pairs of pendulous begonias in hanging baskets on either side of a front door can look formal, through the effect of symmetry. Begonias also reflect the style of their container. The same begonia, for example, can look informal grown in a wicker basket but sedately formal when planted in an ornate terracotta urn.

Grouping begonias Wax begonias are traditionally grown *en masse*, in single or mixed-color strains. In a hanging basket, one fairly big tuberous-rooted begonia is usually enough, but in very large baskets you could plant two or three tubers, in matching or harmonizing flower colors. Foliage begonias, with their subtle contrasts in leaf patterns and shapes, look attractive when they are grouped together in a single container. The larger the begonia, the more effective it is as a specimen plant on its own.

Plant partners Lobelias, petunias, fuchsias, and pelargoniums are the best and most traditional summer partners for begonias, but for a change try alternating wax begonias and ageratum, sweet alyssum or golden feverfew as edging or even for ribbon bedding. In light shade, combine brightly colored begonias and cool-looking ferns. Fill a window box with densely packed wax or tuberous begonias, and add miniature trailing ivy around the edge. You could also edge the base of a pot-grown laurel or fatsia with a row of wax begonias. Indoors, combine velvety-leaved begonias with African violets in a small-scale basket garden.

Color combinations Combine pale pink wax begonias with pale blue lobelia and the silvery foliage of *Helichrysum petiolare* or *Senecio cineraria*. Create an all-white or all-pink container scheme with tuberous-rooted begonias, impatiens, ivy-leaf pelargoniums, and lobelias. Combine bronze-leaved wax begonias with purple-leaved cannas and castor oil plants for a tropical effect.

Popular begonia types

Almost all begonias are essentially indoor or patio plants, and if you want them to flower again in spring they should be brought indoors before the first frosts. If you leave them outside over the winter months they will die.

Wax begonias (*Begonia x semperflorens-cultorum* hybrids) are fibrous-rooted. The wax begonias are the most usual types and can be seen in many parks and gardens. These perennials are grown as half-hardy annuals with red, pink, or white flowers and small, bronze-coloured or green leaves.

Angel wing begonia (*Begonia coccinea*) is a cane-stemmed type with thick, glossy, wing-like leaves and pendulous flowers, which comes in a variety of colors from pink to coral-red. Its flowers appear in spring, and it is best kept indoors.

Begonia evansiana is a tuberous form, with heart-shaped, shiny leaves and pale pink summer flowers. It is most unusual in that it is moderately hardy and can even survive a fairly mild frost, so it can be overwintered outdoors.

Begonia manicata is a rhizomatous type with upright, evergreen leaves which are hairy beneath, and single pink flowers that appear in late winter and early spring. It is best used as a foliage and flowering houseplant.

Eyelash begonia (*Begonia bowerae*) is also rhizomatous and has emerald green, velvety, heart-shaped leaves, edged in black with tiny, pale pink flowers which bloom in winter and early spring.

Hairy leaf begonia (*Begonia metallica*) is a shrubby type, with metallic-green leaves and pale pink or white flowers which are seen in summer and autumn. It makes a good patio plant during the summer months.

Iron cross begonia (*Begonia masoniana*) is a rhizomatous type and has heart-shaped, puckered leaves with a central, maroon-red marking in the shape of a cross. Its single, pale pink summer flowers are rarely produced.

Lorraine begonia (*Begonia cheimantha* "Gloire de Lorraine") is a tuberous type which has evergreen leaves and single, white or pink flowers in winter. This begonia makes an excellent plant for the Christmas season.

Rex, king, or **painted leaf begonia** (*Begonia rex-cultorum* hybrids) is a rhizomatous type and has lovely heart-shaped, evergreen leaves and pale pink flowers that appear in late winter. There are many named hybrids, mostly with variegated leaves.

Tuberous begonias (*Begonia x tuberhybrid* vars.) have large, fleshy leaves and showy male camellia-, rosebud-, or carnation-shaped flowers all on the same plant. Flowers are usually single-colored, but you can obtain bicolored forms, with contrasting margins or blotches. Some types have ruffled petals. Pendulous forms are excellent for planting in hanging baskets. These should be lifted in the fall and overwintered in peat.

Trout begonia (*Begonia argenteoguttata*) is a cane-stemmed type, which has white-spotted, olive-green leaves and pink flowers in spring.

▼ *Garden choice*
Begonia manicata "Crispa" makes unusual ground cover in warm climates or temporary summer bedding in cooler ones. It has wonderfully deep pink flowers and light green leaves

▲ Blaze of color
The popular wax begonia hybrid "Organdy Mixed" is ideal for bedding, window boxes, and flower pots, indoors or out.

▼ Multicolor charm
Tuberous-rooted begonias, including pendulous forms, cascade from a large terracotta pot, bringing color and charm to the steps.

Buying and growing begonias

Buy bedding types after the last frost. Plants in growth should have plenty of buds. Dormant tubers should be plump.

Site outdoors in a warm spot, but avoid a blisteringly hot site —begonias flower profusely in light shade.

Care: From spring to fall, water plants regularly. Take in bedding begonias before the first frost; well cared for, they should last for years. In autumn, withhold water from tuberous types, cut off shoots, then lift and store in peat. Replant them in spring.

Indoors: Site in bright, but indirect light, at a minimum temperature of 45°F (7°C). Virtually all begonias should be overwintered indoors. Prune tall-growing types in spring.

tip

Wax begonia seeds
Mix the tiny wax begonia seeds with fine grains of sand first, then leave the sand and seed mixture exposed on the surface of the potting mix. If they are not disturbed they should root fairly quickly.

▶ *Textured leaves*
The iron cross begonia is grown mainly for its lovely puckered, variegated leaves.

▼ *Striking color*
Pink and green rex begonia leaves, with their colors and abstract patterns, help to create a tropical effect wherever they are positioned.

BEAUTIFUL BUSH ROSES

If you send away for rose catalogs or visit rose growers or flower shows, you'll find that roses are divided into a confusing number of categories, based on breeding, plant structure, and history. Most people, though, simply and sensibly divide roses according to use, as free-standing bushes or climbers needing support. Of the former, hybrid teas and floribundas, with their compact, bushy growth and showy flowers, produced from early summer until the first frost, are all-time favorites.

The pleasures of mixed planting

Hybrid teas and floribundas are often grown in formal, geometrically laid-out beds of single varieties, with carefully tended bare earth beneath. While these can look impressive, even spectacular, the beds take a lot of upkeep and, especially in a small garden, look grim once flowering ends. Except for the choice of variety, they provide no scope for personal style or creativity, and they also lack the natural charm that is an inherent part of country-style gardens.

Nowadays, many people prefer an informal, relaxed approach, with rose bushes, or even a single bush, nestled among herbaceous perennials, annuals, bulbs, and other shrubs in a mixed border. You can still enjoy the beauty of the roses, but can use every bit of planting space, create a uniquely personal scheme, and extend the flowering season from spring into fall by including both early- and late-flowering species. This approach also suits the many modern shrub roses, which include the popular rugosa types, the creamy-white "Nevada," wine-red "Roseraie de l'Hay," and pink-flowered "Queen Elizabeth."

When buying a bush rose, consider not only the flowers and whether they'll fit into your color scheme, but also the flowering time; how reliable they are; the foliage, which can range from dull to a

▲ Orange charm
The main picture shows the unusual coppery orange flowers, veined with red, of hybrid tea "Just Joey." It is scented and grows vigorously.

▲ Heavenly scents
Inset is another hybrid tea, "Peace." Its lovely pale pink, highly scented flowers fit in happily with most country-style gardens.

positive asset; the plant's growth habit; its height; its shape; and its resistance to common rose problems.

Fragrance is an important ingredient of country gardens, so try to choose scented varieties. Many hybrid teas are very fragrant, and of the modern shrub roses, the golden-yellow "Chinatown" and the hybrid musks, such as the pink and ivory "Felicia," are exceptionally fragrant.

Buying and caring for bush roses

Buy containerized roses from garden centers all year round, or bare-rooted roses, bagged in plastic and sometimes boxed, from many sources. The former are more expensive but less risky, and can be planted whenever the ground isn't frozen or waterlogged. (A warning: a gentle tug shows whether a bush rose is truly pot-grown, or bare-rooted and shoved into pots for sale!)

Bagged, bare-rooted roses are less expensive and widely available, but must be planted when dormant; warm store conditions can cause premature growth, dry roots, and shriveled stems. Roses ordered and sent from a specialist nursery also come bare-rooted but should arrive dormant, and well within the planting season.

Check that the bush has two or more plump, bright green stems, at least as thick as a pencil. The roots, if visible, should be fibrous and well developed.

Plant as soon as possible after buying. If you need to delay planting, temporarily plant in a shallow V-shaped trench.

Mulch annually in spring, to keep the soil moist, roots cool, and weeds down and to improve the soil by adding nutrients.

Water whenever the soil is dry.

Prune hybrid teas by removing weak dead and crossing branches above the ground in late autumn or winter.

▶ *Living bouquet*
The delicate white flowers of ornamental seakale surround and enhance these pink floribunda roses, like baby's breath in a bouquet.

▲ Masses of color
The highly scented blooms of this free-flowering hybrid tea, "Pink Peace," are offset by the luxurious, floral blue background.

◄ Cool, calm, and soothing
Even in the heat of summer, these white floribunda roses and mauve hardy geraniums, with their green backdrop, create a cool image.

Plants to grow with roses

There are hundreds of country garden plants that enjoy the sun and the rich, moist, but well-drained soil that suits roses. Lilies, hostas, lady's mantle, delphiniums, campanulas, lupins, iris, peonies, shrubby cinquefoils…the list is almost endless.

For early- and late-season interest, snowdrops, winter aconites, and iris, crocus, alliums, anemones, daffodils, and species tulips tucked among the roses, never fail to please. In early summer, alyssum, aubretia, ajuga and dwarf phlox can form a colorful carpet, helping to keep weeds down at the same time.

Silver is a lovely color with roses, whether one of many artemisias, dusty miller (*Senecio cineraria*), or furry, silver lamb's ears (*Stachys lanata*). Climbers such as honeysuckle or clematis rambling through rose bushes add an informal, rural touch, but be prepared to cut vigorous types back hard.

In densely populated mixed borders, feeding and watering during the growing season are especially important. The occasional clump of foxgloves, delphiniums, or mulleins does no harm, but roses flower best if sunlight can ripen their wood, so don't completely surround them with tall plants.

▼ Something old, something new
In spite of its modern origins, the pink shrub rose "Ballerina," surrounded here by lavender, has an entirely old-fashioned appeal.

▲ Multicolor "Masquerade"
This tall floribunda has bright yellow buds that open pink and mature to a rich crimson, creating a multicolor effect.

▶ A happy compromise
If you like the idea of a rose bed but don't like formality or being limited to one variety, a mixed collection of roses, in a range of colors, edged with low-growing floribundas, is the ideal solution.

tip

The right start in life
Dig a good-sized hole and remove all weeds from the soil and surrounding area. Roses are greedy feeders, so work in plenty of garden compost or pre-bagged, sterilized organic potting mixture, sold at garden centers. Plant firmly and water whenever the weather is dry. Apply multipurpose foliar feed, fungicide, and insecticide in the growing season, according to the instructions.

SPRING BULBS

From delicate, dancing daffodils and sumptuous tulips to heavily fragrant, luxurious hyacinths, flowering bulbs are a glorious source of spring color in the garden.

Once the bulbs are in full bloom, with their showy hues, elegant shapes, and heady fragrance, it means winter is well and truly over and the warm weather is, at last, on its way. Of all spring plants, bulbs are the most versatile. They can be planted in window boxes, flowerpots, and tubs to give a compact display, or they can be simply planted out in the open ground in the grass or placed formally into flower beds. Bulbs look lovely planted either in small, informal clusters or in vast drifts for bedding areas.

Spring bulbs are excellent mixers and can be used to add color and interest to dormant perennial borders or just to complement the first spring perennials, such as the yellow leopard's-bane or blue lungwort blooms. If the bulbs are planted so they are tucked under shrubs, such as camellias, they will add more early color to this section of the garden. Bulbs can be used to liven up any mixed flower borders, generally adding color before most of the perennials flower. Spring bulbs planted in terracotta pots and tubs transform even the most unpromising area of garden or patio into a bright, colorful corner to create a focal point.

Once these plants begin to flower, their heights can range from 2in (5cm) for *Anemone blanda* to 5ft (1.5m) or

▲ Blooming beautiful
Drifts of yellow and white daffodils, white tulips, yellow crown imperial fritillaries, and deep blue bluebells liven up this area of woodland garden spectacularly.

more for crown imperials. Spring bulbs come in virtually every color and shape, including pastels, clear, bright hues, bicolors, and multicolors, and a few have attractive foliage as well. Some prefer hot, dry, sunny spots; others, cool, woodland shade. Whatever the conditions and space available, there are spring bulbs that will thrive in any area of your garden. Wherever you plant them, you will be well-rewarded by their cheerful flowers.

Choosing spring bulbs

Garden centers carry popular spring bulbs, including multi-packs with several types, each separately bagged and labeled. Specialist bulb catalogs offer a wider range of choice, including unusual and challenging types, but you must order them well in advance.

Decide on the site, and eliminate bulbs that are too tall, short, or otherwise unsuitable. Consider the planting style and numbers involved; some types are better for bedding out than others and are sold at a reasonable price, in large quantities. Choosing flower colors, shapes, and possibly fragrance comes next and is enormous fun; but you must consider how the bulbs will look with nearby plants and whether you are prepared to lift the bulbs annually or want a permanent feature.

Using spring bulbs

You can pack many more spring bulbs into a given area than you might think, so if in doubt, buy extra.

Formal or informal Bedding out formally with rows of equally spaced bulbs, or informally interplanted with annuals such as wallflowers calls for sturdy and uniform hybrid varieties, such as Darwin tulips or oriental hyacinth. Species tend to look better in informal clumps or drifts in borders, lawns, or woodland gardens.

Grouping spring bulbs Except for tall, specimen bulbs, such as crown imperial, which can act as a focal point, for the most impact you should plant bulbs in groups. They can be the same variety, mixed colors, or forms of the same genus such as pink and blue hyacinths, or mixed daffodils.

Plant partners Spring bulbs and biennials—sweet Williams, English daisies, and some forget-me-nots—are traditional partners. Among clumps of heather, grow dwarf tulips such as *Tulipa tarda*, *T. kaufmanniana*, or *T. greigii* hybrids, or plant squill among low-growing ornamental thyme. Underplant the early-flowering *Magnolia stellata* with drifts of spring crocus; or yellow-flowered forsythia, mahonia, or kerria with daffodils.

Color combinations All-white schemes are cool and elegant, ideal for formal gardens. Mixed pastels are romantic, and brightly colored mixtures are eye-catching. For a natural effect, select shades and tints of the same color, such as crocuses ranging from white through lilac, lavender, and deep purple, planted in a lawn.

Popular spring bulbs

Anemone (*Anemone*) has bowl-shaped, white, pink, blue, red, purple, or bi-color flowers. Plant in moist soil.

Crocuses (*Crocus*) have goblet-shaped, white, yellow, purple, or bicolored flowers. They like well-drained soil and are excellent for planting in grass.

Dogtooth violet (*Erythronium*) has lily-like flowers in pink, yellow, or white, and marbled leaves. The violet likes moist soil and shade.

Glory-of-the-snow (*Chionodoxa luciliae*) has spikes of blue, pink, or white flowers. Plant in well-drained soil.

Fritillary (*Fritillaria*) has drooping, bell-shaped flowers—yellow or reddish in *F. imperialis*, checkered red and white in *F. meleagris*.

tip

Picking bulb flowers
When cutting blooms for indoor displays, it is a good idea to leave the lower white stem attached to the bulb, to provide nourishment for next year's flowering.

▶ **Spring delight**
The wood hyacinth (Hyacinthoides hispanica) *finds a shady home under this flowering azalea. The new growth on the two plants brings a burst of color into the garden.*

▼ **A patch of white**
The dogtooth violet "White Beauty," *set against its own attractive foliage, enhances an otherwise all-green area of the garden.*

Grape hyacinth (*Muscari*) has spikes of tiny, tightly packed blue flowers. It likes well-drained soil and sun.

Hyacinth (*Hyacinthus*) has densely packed, fragrant, bell-shaped pink, white, cream, or blue flowers on leafless stalks. Plant in well-drained soil.

Daffodils (*Narcissus*) have yellow, white, or bicolored blooms, some with orange "trumpets." Plant in well-drained soil.

Flowering onion (*Allium*) has globe-shaped heads of small flowers, pink in *A. karataviense*, yellow in *A. moly*, white in *A. neapolitanum*.

Squill (*Scilla*) has spikes of bell-shaped, usually blue, flowers on bare stems. It likes moist soil.

Tulip (*Tulipa*) has goblet or star-shaped blooms. Plant to suit type; light soil for species; well-drained for hybrids.

► *Chic checks*
*The elegant blooms of the checkered lily (*Fritillaria meleagris*) look almost as if they were made from pink-and-white checked fabric. The bulb is quite hardy but prefers moist, rich soil. In England it is called the snake's head fritillary.*

▼ *Bell of the ball*
Set amid dancing daffodils and red tulips, the Siberian squill has found an ideal home. It likes damp soil and is a hardy plant, with vibrant blue nodding star-like flowers.

▲ Lasting display
Hyacinths are hardy plants and look excellent grouped in clumps for beds and borders. This hyacinth "Delft Blue" can either be forced for indoor color or planted out in the fall. If planted, bulbs usually flower for successive years if the winters are mild.

► Colorful trio
Grape hyacinths are very easy bulbs to grow and are excellent for naturalizing, as, once planted, they multiply freely. Here, grape hyacinths join trumpet daffodils and sprigs of purple-leaved hazel "Purpurea" to form an eye-catching combination.

tip

Window boxes
It is important to use bulbs that do not need depth to root. Good options include crocus species, *Anemone blanda*, or the miniature *Narcissus triandrus albus* "Angel's Tears."

CLIMBING CLEMATIS

Clematis are excellent partners for each other— or for different climbers such as honeysuckle or roses—because their foliage is not smothering. They come in a range of flowering periods and colors. Here, "Nelly Moser" and "Alice Fisk" combine for a glorious midsummer display.

▲ Tree climbers
Large-flowered clematis provide unexpected pleasure when grown up and through the branches of a small tree. Plant on the north side of the trunk, so the clematis roots are in shade, and lead the stems to the tree branches with a stout cane.

Clematis, with its enchanting flowers, silky seed heads, and charming informality, is a much-loved feature of country gardens. Luckily, its rural charm travels well, and clematis thrives in town gardens, in containers as well as open ground.

Most clematis species have twining leaf stalks that curl around the nearest support, whether another plant or an artificially provided trellis, while a few drape themselves over the ground.

These plants are usually deciduous, flowering in late spring and summer, but there are fall- and winter-flowering types, as well as evergreen species for warm, sheltered spots in the garden.

Choosing a clematis

The flowers range from the subtle to the spectacular and come in white, shades of pink, scarlet, crimson, wine, blue, mauve, and violet. There are also yellow- and green-flowered clematis, and bicolored ones, with contrasting stripes or inner petals. (Technically, clematises have colored sepals, rather than petals.) In some, the central stamens are a feature, in others, the seed heads that follow the flowers are prized.

Blooms can be single, semi-double, or double, cup- or bell-shaped, and range from ½in to 10in (12mm–25cm) or more across. A few, such as the red-tinged, violet-blue "Vyvyan Pennell," bloom twice a year, the first flush double, and the later flush single. Flowers can face toward the sun or hang down, an important factor in siting clematis. Ideally, you should look up into pendent blooms and straight at or down onto upward-facing ones. If they are way above your head, only the undersides of clematis blooms show.

If you're partnering a clematis with another plant, consider the pruning needs of both plants. You don't want to train a clematis that needs no pruning, for example, over a hybrid tea rose that has to be cut back hard every year. Also consider the vigor of each plant: strong-growing clematises can swamp small shrubs such as daphne or potentilla.

If you have lots of spring and summer color but your garden looks bare during the rest of the year, try to fit in a fall- or winter-flowering clematis. You could plant snowdrops and helle-bores around the base for winter interest. For an autumn-flowering clematis, such as the yellow *Clematis orientalis* or *Clematis tangutica*, you could plant the brilliant blue-flowered hardy plumbago, or a pale blue globe-shaped hydrangea in front, to shade the clematis roots and provide informal support.

Decorative ideas

Because clematis plants have no real form of their own, they take the shape of their support, although the flowers and foliage often mound up attractively on the top of a trellis or roof. Most clematis foliage is dull, so visually "borrowing" nearby foliage, or growing it through a tree or shrub, is a good idea.

Natural supports Train vigorous varieties up tall trees; compact species up fruit trees or over tree stumps.

Formal effects Grow clematis in free-standing tubs with a pyramid or fan-shaped trellis attached.

Flowering tepees In mixed borders support clematis, English cottage-garden style, on branches or poles stuck into the ground and formed into a roughly pyramidal or tepee shape.

As ground cover Grow clematis as it grows in the wild, over banks and mounds, but first make sure the soil is weed-free.

Pergola partners Train clematis and roses up an arbor or pergola.

"Borrowed" foliage Plant clematis next to a shrub, such as box or laurustinus (*Viburnum tinus*), to grow up and through it.

▲ **Clematis camouflage**
Clematis montana *is an especially vigorous climber. It grows fast, quickly forming an attractive disguise for unsightly toolsheds or walls.*

◄ **A clematis-framed welcome**
Clematises are excellent for training on pergolas or on house walls around doorways and windows. Here "Ville de Lyon," one of the many large-flowered hybrids, provides a magnificent show.

▶ **Bench occupied**
A vibrant "Lasurstern" clematis seedling takes advantage of a vacant space on a garden bench.

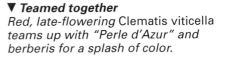

▼ *Teamed together*
Red, late-flowering Clematis viticella *teams up with "Perle d'Azur" and berberis for a splash of color.*

Cultivating clematis
Buying plants in flower eliminates disappointment, but always read the label attached: two different varieties with almost identical flowers can vary dramatically in eventual height and vigor.
Site: Clematis roots need cool shade, and the top growth should reach sunlight, although pale-colored forms prefer light shade.
Plant in rich moist neutral or alkaline soil.
Support: Clematises are self-supporting, provided they have an open framework to cling to. A bare wall is not suitable. Use trellis, netting, or closely spaced wires.
Care: In full sun, mulch or plant low-growing plants in front, or cover roots with a paving slab. Prune early-flowering species after flowering, if necessary. Prune species flowering on new wood in late winter. Prune early-flowering hybrids lightly in late winter; prune those flowering from midsummer back to 3ft (1m) above ground in late winter.

Popular clematis types

There are hundreds of different clematis varieties; garden centers carry a good range, and for the enthusiast there are specialist clematis nurseries. Basically, the species and their varieties, such as *Clematis alpina* and *Clematis montana* var. *rubens*, are easy to grow and range from 6 to 60ft (1.8–18m) high. The popular, large-flowered hybrids, such as *Clematis* "Comtesse de Bouchaud" and "Jackmanii Superba," are 8–15ft (2.5–4.5m) high, often with spectacular flowers, but they can be tricky to grow.

Early- and mid-spring flowers *Clematis armandii*, growing to 20ft (6m), has glossy evergreen leaves and white flowers—pink and white in the variety "Apple Blossom," with bronze young foliage. *Clematis alpina*, grows to 6ft (1.8m) high, and has bell-like, violet-blue flowers, followed by silky seed heads.

▼ Silky seed heads
In addition to its lovely yellow, lantern-shaped flowers, Clematis tangutica *produces particularly interesting seed heads.*

◄ Informal scrambling
Although they are usually trained up supports, clematises also look lovely scrambling informally over whatever lies in their way, just as they do in the wild.

▼ A bushy prop
Clematises tend to take the shape of their support. This perennial border hosts a radiant "John Huxtable," which has swathed itself over a shrub.

Late spring and early summer flowers *Clematis macropetala*, growing to 8ft (2.5m), has semi-double violet flowers, pink in the variety "Markham's Pink," followed by silky seed heads. *Clematis montana* is one of the easiest species, and tolerates acid soils. Growing up to 40ft (12m) high, it has masses of white flowers, pink in the variety *rubens*.

Midsummer and autumn flowers *Clematis orientalis*, the orange-peel clematis, reaches 20ft (6m) high and has fragrant flowers with thick, orange-yellow sepals, followed by silky seed pods. The sweet autumn clematis (*C. paniculata*) produces masses of small, white fragrant blooms in late summer and early fall; it is one of the easiest clematises to grow.

PLANTS FOR SUNNY GARDENS

Some gardens are sun traps; others have south-facing walls which catch the sun almost all day. These areas need sun-loving plants. If you are lucky enough to have an area like this, your gardening options are almost unlimited. A well-planned sunny border or corner can be stunning, while a whole garden filled with sun-loving plants is a potential paradise of colorful flowers and attractive green foliage.

Sun-loving plants range from alpine saxifrages, less than 1in (2.5cm) high, to huge trees, such as the snow gum (*Eucalyptus gunnii*). Most annuals and tender bedding plants are sun-loving, and there are sun-loving biennials, such as sweet Williams; herbaceous perennials, such as delphiniums; and both evergreen and deciduous shrubs. Many different colored-leaved shrubs, such as smoke bush (*Cotinus coggygria*), with its luxuriant purple foliage, thrive in sun;

▲ Basic blues
Hardy herbaceous geraniums in blue and fuchsia, catmint, and lavender are combined in this mature, sun-filled summer border.

and color schemes can range from brilliant tropical reds, purples, and hot pinks to subtle silvers, grays, and whites. Flowers can be almost any shape and size, but the daisy, or Compositae family, which includes daisies, dahlias, asters, sunflowers, achilleas, cosmos, senecios, artemisias, cornflowers, knapweeds, zinnias, and French marigolds, is well represented among sun-lovers.

Flowers such as bergenia, lady's mantle, or geraniums which are happy in sun or shade tend to bloom earlier in full sun; provided their needs for food and water are met, they will produce flowers long after similar plants in shady spots have finished.

Choosing sun-loving plants
Decide whether you want a temporary or long-lived, deciduous or evergreen plant, and the approximate width, height, and shape of the fully grown plant. Consider the color scheme of any nearby plants and when you want the display season to be. Many sun-loving plants are seen only during the spring and summer, but some, such as *Nerine bowdenii*, bloom in the fall whereas others, like winter aconites (*Eranthis hyemalis*), bloom during the winter months.

Silver-leaved and succulent sun-loving plants need dry, average, or poor soil, while others, such as ragwort, thrive in rich, damp, almost boggy conditions but most plants are happy somewhere between the two. Some sun-lovers, such as heather, are tolerant of exposure, while others, such as lupins, need some shelter during the hottest weeks of the year.

Ways with sun-loving plants

Formal or informal Summer bedding schemes are the traditional example of sun-loving flowers used formally, while informal, old-fashioned gardens, with a glorious muddle of plants and flowers, are the other extreme. The same flowers—petunias or lobelias, for example—can be successfully used in either type of garden, although for formal bedding, choose recommended cultivars and hybrids that are reliably compact and uniform in their growth habit, flower color, and overall height.

Grouping sun-loving plants Perennial borders filled with sun-loving plants are delightful, but it is easier to achieve an ongoing seasonal display with a mixed border containing pockets of bulbs, biennials, and annuals, as well as a permanent framework of shrubs. Either way, try to plant groups of three or five of each type of plant and include plenty of ground-cover plants, such as hardy geraniums with attractive, weed-proof leaves, to minimize maintenance and provide interest when the bulbs are not in flower.

Color schemes A silver and gray border is one traditional type of scheme, with lavender, lavender cotton, various artemisias, cineraria, globe thistles, and perhaps even a few globe artichokes for back-of-the-border height. Pastel schemes based on pinks and blues are lovely and are suitable for border and bedding out, as are hot schemes, based on clashing reds, oranges, and yellows. Monochromatic schemes, in shades of all blue, all pink, all yellow, or all white can be very striking; many sun-loving plants, such as agapanthus and campanula, can easily be bought in most colors or in white-flowered forms.

Plant partnerships You can combine lavender cotton, purple-leaf culinary sage, and pinks for an effective soft, purple, pink, and white scheme. Try also combining yuccas, rockrose, and lavender; or bergenia, pearly everlasting (*Anaphalis margaritacea*), and epimediums, for a scheme using contrasting color and leaf forms. For a pretty pastel scheme, combine pink roses, lacy-leaved rue, and blue pansies; or pink peonies, blue iris, and culinary sage. A simple but striking blue and yellow scheme can easily be achieved by combining daylilies and catmint; or, for a vertical splash of color, combine climbing morning glories and nasturtiums.

▶ **In the pink**
"The Page," a Russell lupin seed strain in shades of carmine, is a short-lived perennial favored in English cottage gardens.

▶ **Brilliant red**
The oriental poppy "Goliath" is a rather sprawling, clump-forming herbaceous perennial, but it is also one of the most popular border plants, at its best during the early summer months. The foliage should be cut back hard after flowering if you want to produce new growth the next year. In warm zones you may even see some flowers in winter, but these will be short-lived.

▲ Regal gold
Achillea "Coronation Gold" is a long-lasting perennial, excellent for use in fresh and dried flower displays.

▼ Rainbow display
Phlox, achillea, loosestrife, and campanulas create a brilliant, multicolored border.

Popular sun-loving plants

The following are just a few of the many plants that thrive in full sun.

Alpine plants suitable for a sunny spot include heather, dwarf conifers, rockrose, aubretia, alyssum, sempervivum, fleabane, and saxifrages.

Annuals are almost too numerous to mention but include petunias, sweet alyssum, begonia, ageratum, cosmos, zinnia, California poppy, candytuft, cornflower, morning glory, nasturtium, and African and French marigolds.

Biennials for sun include polyanthus, wallflower, sweet Williams, mullein, evening primrose, Canterbury bells, English daisy, forget-me-not, foxglove, and hollyhocks.

Herbaceous perennials are old-time summer favorites. Delphiniums, lupins, campanula, scabious, phlox, globe thistle, poppy, goldenrod, catmint, baby's breath, achillea, acanthus, bearded iris, lamb's-ears, and peonies are sun-lovers.

Shrubs include rose, ceanothus, cistus, lilac, rue, lavender, broom, Mexican orange, potentilla, rosemary, and thyme. Glossy abelia, Russian olive, and shrubby artemisias are good for foliage schemes.

Climbing plants include ornamental vines such as Virginia creeper and Boston ivy. Japanese wisteria needs sun in order for its beautiful flowers to develop.

Flowering bulbs include tulip, hyacinth, crocus, daffodil, and grape hyacinth for spring; agapanthus, gladiolus, tuberous-rooted begonia, and allium.

Buying and caring for sun-loving plants

Buy woody plants, perennials, and alpines in pots when the ground is suitable for planting. Buy trays of annuals or bedding plants in early summer, and most biennials and bulbs in early autumn. Choose compact, healthy plants with buds and plump bulbs that are free of pests or diseases.

Site: Choose ordinary, rich, or poor soil, moist or dry, according to the plant. Most sun-lovers will thrive in fairly dry soil.

Plant firmly in weed-free, well-dug soil, enriched with organic matter. Water in dry weather, according to the plant's needs.

Cultivation and care: Feed in spring and summer. Stake tall-growing types. Protect from slugs and insect pests. Deadhead, and cut back perennials such as delphiniums after flowering, to promote a second crop of flowers. Cut back herbaceous perennials in mid-autumn to ground level, and protect against frost if necessary. Lift, divide, and replant perennials every 3–5 years.

▲ *Sunny side up*
*The quick-growing annual sunflower (*Helianthus annuus*) makes an unusual screen, and birds love its seeds.*

▼ *California poppy*
Eschscholzia californica is a self-seeding annual. The petals close at night but open in the sun.

PLANTS FOR SHADE

A shady garden can be every bit as beautiful as a sunny one. A surprising number of popular plants tolerate, or actually prefer, shade.

Most gardens have at least one shady patch or corner, whether it be solid shade from an adjacent house or boundary walls, or the dappled, seasonal shade from deciduous trees or large shrubs. A few gardens are fully shaded, most if not all of the time. Whatever the degree or amount of shade your garden has, you can turn it to your advantage by choosing the right plants.

Shade-loving plants come in a wide range of types, including ground-cover plants, such as lily-of-the-valley, and other herbaceous perennials, such as aquilegia, hellebores, and bergenias; bulbs, such as anemones and bluebells; shrubs, such as pieris, skimmia, and aucuba; and trees, such as yew and holly. Many plants known for their sun-loving natures—roses, for example—include a few varieties that perform perfectly well in shade, flowering for months on end. Ask at your garden center for details.

There are both evergreen and deciduous shade-loving plants, shade-loving annuals and bedding plants, such as impatiens and tender fuchsias; and some of the most stunning of all garden flowers—camellias, clematis, and rhododendrons—also love shade.

Variegated plants with white-spotted, striped, or splashed leaves, such as some ivies, hostas, and impatiens, are at their best grown in shade, while ferns, with their delicate fronds, can partner shade-loving flowering and foliage plants, or form a subtle ground cover.

▲ **Shady border**
Clipped topiary balls, campanulas, foxgloves, and climbing roses fill this shady border.

Choosing plants for shade
Decide on the space or area available, including maximum height; whether you want a few large plants or several smaller ones; and whether you want permanent trees and shrubs, relatively long-lived perennials, or plants, such as annuals and bedding, that need regular replacement. Consider leaf, stem, and flower color in relation to nearby plants. Think of seasonal impact—you may want a fall or winter display, when the rest of the garden is dull, or an evergreen one for year-round cover.

Consider, too, soil type and exposure; a shady, sheltered spot with rich, moisture-retentive soil can accommodate a wider range of plants than a shady, windy one with poor, dry soil. Shade from a tree crown, coupled with greedy, shallow tree roots and dry soil, is especially challenging.

If you are using containers—say for a shady patio or balcony—you can match the potting soil to the plants: ericaceous compost for camellias, rhododendrons, and pieris, for example, and high-nutrient loam-based types for herbaceous perennials.

Ways with shade-loving plants

Formal or informal Clipped dwarf box hedging can mark out geometric beds filled with shade-loving plants. Topiary box, holly, or bay in a pot can stand sentry outside a front door or garden gate, and shade-loving firethorn can be wall-trained around a door.

You can grow shade-loving plants informally in a woodland garden, in borders, or as intermingling ground cover; or you can underplant a late-leafing tree, such as hazel, with drifts of primroses, bluebells, and forget-me-nots.

Grouping shade-lovers As a general rule, groups of three, five, or seven of a single type of plant are more effective than individual plants dotted about. Try to contrast growth habit and leaf size, shape, and texture as well as color: the comparative silhouettes and light-reflecting or absorbing qualities of clumps of plants can create interest.

Using colors Pale tints, such as pastel pink, blue, apricot, mauve, and yellow and white, show up better in shade than rich, dark tones, which visually recede.

An all-year, all-white floral scheme, based on snowdrops, camellias, and hellebores in winter; white rhododendrons, Solomon's seal, and lilies-of-the-valley in spring; white roses, peonies, and campanulas in summer; and autumnal white hydrangeas and Japanese anemones can be stunning. You can extend the white theme with variegated foliage. Group different cultivars of hostas—some with green centers and white edging, others the reverse—for an impressive display.

Variegated evergreens, such as holly, pittosporum, ivy, and elaeagnus offer excellent value, providing two or more colors all year round.

▲ Double value
The shrubby Hypericum inodorum *"Elstead" carries flowers and fruits together in summer and fall.*

Popular shade-loving plants

Bergenia (*Bergenia* spp. and var.) is an evergreen perennial with large, leathery, glossy leaves and spikes of pink flowers, which appear in the spring.

Camellia (*Camellia* spp. and var.) is an evergreen shrub with white, pink, or red single, semi-double, or double flowers from fall to spring. Choose areas with neutral or acid soil for the plant.

Campanula (*Campanula* spp. and var.) is an herbaceous perennial suitable for rock gardens or borders. Depending on the species, it has spikes, clusters, or mounds of bell- or star-shaped blooms, mostly blue, but also found in pink or white.

Clematis (*Clematis* spp. and hybrids) is a climber, with blue, purple, pink, white, or red single or double, flat-faced, cup- or bell-shaped blooms, which appear in spring, summer, and autumn. It likes neutral or alkaline, cool soil that doesn't dry out.

Cyclamen (*C. hederifolium*) is a tuber, hardy in zones 7–9, with heart-shaped leaves, marbled green and white, and elegant pink or white flowers with swept-back petals, seen in autumn and winter. Choose a well-drained soil for the plants.

Cranesbill (*Geranium* spp. and var.) is a clump-forming, hardy herbaceous

◄ Sweet scent
Lilies-of-the-valley can form a dense ground cover and perfume the spring air with their heady scent.

perennial, best for border or rock gardens. It has pretty lobed or cut leaves, often with good autumn color and blue, magenta, pink, or white, saucer-shaped blooms, seen in spring and summer. It makes excellent weed-proof ground cover.

Hellebore (*Helleborus* spp., var., and hybrids) is an evergreen, or semi-evergreen perennial with lance-shaped, toothed, often leathery leaflets; thick-petaled, long-lasting, bowl-shaped blooms in late winter and early spring, in white, green, pink, and subtle purples. Plant in well-drained, rich soil. This plant is good for container growing or for planting in damp areas, near ornamental pools, for example.

Hosta (*Hosta* spp., var., and hybrids) is a clump-forming, hardy herbaceous perennial, with lance-shaped to round green, gold, gray, or variegated leaves, and spikes of modest white or mauve flowers in summer. It likes rich, moisture-retentive soil.

Impatiens (*Impatiens walleriana* hybrids) is a tender, bushy perennial grown as an annual; it has oval green or variegated leaves and single or double pink, white, orange, or purple flowers all summer long. Plant in a cool area.

Lily-of-the-valley (*Convallaria majalis*) is a spreading rhizome with pairs of spear-shaped leaves and spikes of fragrant bell-shaped blooms which appear in spring or early summer. It likes moist, well-drained soil.

Rhododendron (*Rhododendron* spp., var., and hybrids) is a hardy, mostly evergreen shrub with dark-green, oval leaves, and showy flowers which appear singly or in clusters, in all colors but true blue. Deciduous types (commonly known as azaleas) often have attractive spring and autumn leaf color, and some are fragrant. Plant in moist soil on a lime-free site.

St. John's wort (*Hypericum* spp., var., and hybrids) is an herbaceous perennial with oval, aromatic leaves; showy yellow blooms in summer with, or followed by, red fruit in some varieties. Plant in ordinary, well-drained soil.

▲ *Oriental splendor*
*The long-lived Lenten rose (*Helleborus orientalis*), carries dusky, deep pink flowers, which usually appear early in spring.*

▼ *Lively duo*
The gray Hosta sieboldiana *and variegated* Hosta undulate *add lively color and form, making an interesting addition to this border.*

146

Shady business

Shady walls and corners where two walls meet offer rewards as well as challenges. The shelter from a wall protects plants from cold or drying winds. Even north-facing walls retain a few degrees of heat absorbed during the day, providing a little protection.

The soil at the base of a wall tends to be dry because of overhead gutters, coping, foundations, and the rain shadow of the wall itself. Prepare the soil thoroughly, adding plenty of well-rotted organic matter, and water generously until the plants are established, and thereafter in hot, dry weather. Always plant at least lft (30cm) from a wall.

Clematis are shady wall favorites, and are especially free-flowering if the upper stems catch the sun, but roses, winter-flowering jasmine, honeysuckle, climbing hydrangea, and Virginia creeper are all reliable climbers for shady walls. For wall-trained shrubs, choose camellia, quinces (*Chaen-omeles*), with their pretty spring blossom and bright yellow fruits, or *Eunymous fortunei radicans*, which is evergreen and comes in a wealth of variegated forms.

▲ Under cover
Hardy Cyclamen hederifolium *can thrive under trees and produce a striking display year after year.*

▼ Leafy corner
Pansies, geraniums, and clematis blooms add touches of late spring color to a shady garden corner.

tip

Enlivening the setting
To enhance a shady courtyard, paint the surrounding brick walls white and spot or flood-light them at night.

TREES FOR SMALL GARDENS

Trees add an extra dimension to a garden; in a small garden, a single tree can make the difference between a dull plot and an inviting, leafy haven.

However small your garden, it's bound to benefit from the presence of a well-chosen tree. A tree's size, compared to shrubs and flowers, and its vertical contrast to lawns, patios, and flower beds, make it an automatic focal point, and the color and form of its leaves, flowers, and fruits often set the seasonal tone for the entire garden. On a practical level, even a small tree can provide shelter, shade, and privacy—especially important if your garden backs onto others and is overlooked. On a new or bare plot, a tree can create a quick sense of permanence, especially if it is visible from outside the garden.

Trees are basically woody plants with a bare, straight stem branching at the top, although some trees such as magnolia can be multi-stemmed, and some shrubs, such as rhododendron, can reach tree-like size. Tree heights can reach 100ft (30m) or more, in the case of the sugar maple, but the best trees for small gardens are mostly 10–20ft (3–6m) high.

There are evergreen and deciduous compact trees, flowering in spring, summer, fall, or winter, according to type. Some have a picturesque growth habit, others have colorful new spring foliage, fantastic autumn leaf color, or ornamental fruits, while a few, such as the flowering crab apple, have several seasonal features, including fruit for preserves.

▲ Traditional charm
The quince (Cydonia oblonga) is a traditional favorite in Europe, and is ideal for small, sheltered gardens. It has pretty pink or white flowers in spring and is also known for its lightly fragrant fruit, which is used to make jams and jellies.

Choosing trees
Flowering trees are always popular, but generally, the smaller the garden, the more important it is that the tree has several seasons of interest. Find out if it flowers or fruits when young and if male or female species are necessary for flowering; a garden center will be able to advise you. Also consider the length and reliability of the display season. With deciduous trees, always consider

their appearance throughout the winter.

Consider growth rate; some Japanese maples take twenty years or more to reach their final size, whereas eucalyptus can be very quick indeed. Always consider your garden's soil, aspect, and shelter in relation to the tree's needs. Also check that the cultivar name on the label is what you want, and if in doubt, ask; varieties of one tree type can vary enormously in potential size.

If you have small children, avoid laburnums, as their seeds are poisonous. Willows can undermine foundations so shouldn't be planted in small gardens. There are no specific rules regarding the height of the tree in relation to its distance from the house, but obviously light and space requirements are important.

For truly instant effect, you can buy extra-large nursery stock or semi-mature trees from specialist suppliers. Such trees are costly and require special care.

▲ *Early show*
*The profuse lavender-pink flowers of the Judas tree (*Cercis siliquastrum*) appear on the dark, leafless branches in mid-spring.*

Ways with trees
In small gardens, with house and boundary walls, manhole covers, and underground drains and cables to consider, potential tree sites are limited. Decide whether you want to see the tree from the main rooms of the house or use it to hide a view of a busy street. For formality, plant a pair of trees on either side of a gate, steps, or door; or train a pair of laburnums over an arch.

In a small courtyard garden, you can make the tree the center of a circular brickwork or paving scheme, or build a circular seat around the tree, for emphasis. Even placing a bench or garden statue under a tree can create a

handsome double feature, with each adding to the other.

Siting a tree in the middle of the garden is traditional, but placing it on one side or as the high point of a mixed border can be more interesting. Illuminating a tree can create a highly dramatic, nighttime effect, especially if it is lit from below. The tree's beauty can be enjoyed from inside the house as well as from the garden itself; for temporary lighting for a summer party, string white Christmas-tree lights through the branches.

Plant partners

Underplanting trees in lawns with bulbs such as crocuses, bluebells, or daffodils creates a pretty, meadow garden effect, especially if these are combined with primroses or other wildflowers. For masses of attractive, often marbled foliage and dainty pink or white flowers from fall to spring (in zones 7–9), plant hardy cyclamen under a tree. They thrive and multiply even in the driest, shadiest, root-infested soil.

A tree in a border can be underplanted with shade-tolerant shrubs or flowers in harmonizing or contrasting colors. For example, you could plant white wake-robin (*Trillium grandiflorum*) under a flowering cherry tree. A laburnum, with its yellow blossom, underplanted with campanulas and iris, in tints of blue also looks lovely. Another idea is to train a clematis, honeysuckle, or climbing rose up a tree.

Popular small garden trees

Allegheny serviceberry (*Amelanchier laevis*) has a spreading growth habit with bronze leaves and white flowers in spring.
Autumn-flowering cherry (*Prunus subhirtella* var. *autumnalis*) has pink semi-double flowers in spring and fall and striking autumn leaf color.

Eastern redbud (*Cercis canadensis*) is one of the prettiest of the spring-flowering trees, bearing deep red buds which open into rose-pink flowers.
English holly (*Ilex aquifolium* "Argentea Marginata Pendula") has a weeping growth habit and silver-edged, evergreen leaves with red berries in fall.
Fig (*Ficus carica*) is a multi-stemmed tree with a picturesque growth habit and large, lobed leaves with silvery-gray bark and edible fruits. To encourage fruiting, restrict roots.
Golden chain (*Laburnum x watereri* "Vossii") has yellow flowers in spring and poisonous seeds. Plant in a shady site.
Japanese dogwood (*Cornus kousa*) provides masses of white flowers in early summer, scarlet foliage in autumn, and attractively mottled bark in winter. It is more disease-resistant than the traditional favorite *C. florida*.
Japanese maple (*Acer japonicum*

Saving the label

If a tree turns out to be mislabeled or if it dies before it becomes established, take the tree and its label back to the place you bought it. You'll find that most reputable garden centers will replace the plant free of charge during the appropriate season or refund your money.

▲ Luscious blooms
Magnolia x soulangeana *makes an elegant, multi-stemmed tree, with fragrant, waxy blooms in spring. It is excellent for small gardens, especially if placed in a central bed.*

◄ Double bonus
*The staghorn sumach (*Rhus typhina*) has fiery autumn colors and, on the female trees, velvety fruits, which are attractive and last throughout the winter.*

► Autumnal gold
*Instead of the orange berries typical of the European rowan (*Sorbus aucuparia*), "Joseph Rock" has pale yellow berries which remain long after the leaves fall.*

Buying and caring for trees

Buy container-grown trees all year round, but ideally in spring or fall. Bare-rooted trees, should be bought when dormant, from late fall to early spring. Choose compact trees, with balanced crowns. Avoid any with wilted leaves or signs of disease or pests.

Site in an area with sun or light shade according to type. In general, early-flowering trees prefer shelter and later-flowering trees, or those with autumn color, prefer an area with well-drained soil.

Plant containerized trees whenever the ground isn't frozen or waterlogged, and bare-rooted trees when dormant, in weed-free, well-dug soil, enriched with well-rotted organic matter. The top of the rootball should be level with the surrounding soil. Stake and tie, using plastic ties.

Care: Weed the area regularly, and water in dry weather for the first three growing seasons. Check newly planted trees and re-firm if lifted by frost. Mulch with well-rotted organic matter in spring. Remove stake and ties once firmly established. Prune to remove dead, diseased, and awkwardly placed branches in late winter or early spring. Water trees in tubs regularly, especially in hot weather, as they will dry out quickly.

▼ Slow-growing
The golden Japanese maple (Acer japonicum "Aureum") takes many years to make a graceful, spreading tree, but it is worth the wait.

► Strawberry tree
Arbutus unedo, a picturesque evergreen tree, has lily-of-the-valley-like flowers and red-and-yellow, but flavorless cherry-like fruits.

"Aureum") has a wide-spreading growth with young yellow leaves which become green as they mature. It shows red flowers in spring.

Magnolia (*Magnolia x soulangiana*) is a multi-stemmed tree with tulip-shaped white and rosy-red flowers and very handsome seed pods. Choose a sheltered but not too shady site.

Ornamental crab apple (*Malus x* "Red Jewel") has white flowers in spring and bears small, bright red fruit used for jams and jellies.

Quince (*Cydonia oblonga*) has a picturesque growth habit and white or pink flowers and large pear-shaped fruit.

Silver-leafed pear (*Pyrus salicifolia* "Pendula") has a weeping willow-like growth habit and small white flowers.

Snow gum (*Eucalyptus niphophila*) is an evergreen with aromatic, gray-green leaves and attractive, green and white bark. It has white flowers in summer.

Staghorn sumach (*Rhus typhina*) is a wide-spreading tree with large, fern-like leaves and brilliant autumn color; it bears long-lasting, crimson fruits.

Strawberry tree (*Arbutus unedo*) has a picturesque, multi-stemmed growth habit, evergreen leaves, and attractive red peeling bark. It bears white flowers in late summer, red-and-yellow fruit in fall.

4
THE INDOOR COUNTRY GARDEN

GROWING FOR CUTTING

For country-fresh arrangements at a fraction of florists' prices, grow your own flowers and foliage for cutting.

Picking and arranging flowers from your own garden is a traditional country pastime, as gratifying today as in more leisurely days gone by. By growing your own material for cutting, you can create truly personalized displays with your favorite colors and scents, as well as being able to include varieties not available at florists' stores. You can pick material at the optimum stage of growth, condition it correctly, and get it into water quickly, ensuring a long-lasting show. By trading material with friends,

you can enlarge your palette further.

Years ago, when most gardens were bigger than those of today, flowers for cutting were grown in special beds—often in the kitchen garden. These days, in more compact gardens, it's easy to incorporate flowers and foliage for cutting in mixed beds and borders; with careful planning, you can cut flowers and foliage to your heart's content, without leaving the garden bare.

Material suitable for cutting includes annuals, such as larkspur and love-in-a-mist; biennials, such as forget-me-nots and wallflowers; perennials, such as peonies and delphiniums; bulbs,

▲ Creative choice
Home-grown flowers provide far and away the best range of raw material from which to choose, and since they are almost literally grown on your doorstep, they are also convenient.

such as tulips and hyacinths; shrubs, such as roses and camellias; and even trees, such as ornamental cherries and crab apples. Rock gardens provide sprigs for miniature floral displays; herb gardens have aromatic or feathery foliage; and walls can be used to grow ivy and honeysuckle, which will add a sense of movement to flower displays.

Choosing plants

Go for flower colors that match your decor or for neutral creams and white; try to choose reliable plants, fragrant if possible, with a long flowering season from a young age. Foliage is valuable for creating generously full displays; evergreen foliage is especially valuable from late autumn until mid-spring, and variegated foliage, as found in some varieties of holly, elaeagnus, eunymous and even privet, is worth its weight in gold. Consider a plant's potential display life indoors; ceanothus, for example, flowers for weeks in the garden, but quickly and irreversibly wilts when cut.

Try to include late-fall, winter, and early spring flowers, such as hellebores and camellias. If you have a small garden, concentrate on a good selection of foliage to bulk out florists' flowers. And, as always, consider a plant's soil, light, shelter, and space needs; how tough or demanding a nature it has, and how its appearance will affect the existing garden scheme.

▼ Numbers count
The larger the group of one type of flower, the easier it will be to harvest flowers without leaving gaps. Here, massed lilies edged with hyssop create a good picking display.

Cut flowers in the garden

Formal or informal Almost any garden style can incorporate flowers for cutting. You can grow flowers in rows in formal rectangular, circular, or free-form beds, or in informal clustered groups, here and there, English cottage-garden style. The more relaxed and generously full the scheme is, however, the easier it will be to cut flowers without creating any obvious gaps in the garden.

Grouping flowers for cutting Use the same guidelines that you would for ordinary garden layouts: contrasting forms, sizes, and textures, ideally with a sequential display, one plant coming into season as another finishes.

Color ideas Almost any successful color scheme outdoors can be transferred indoors: mixed bright colors; mixed pastels, bicolored schemes, such as blue and yellow, and monochromatic schemes, ranging from pale to deep of a single hue, or plain white. Seasonal changes of color themes, from the palest pastels of spring to the richest oranges, and flame-reds of autumn, are as welcome in the house as in the garden.

Non-floral material In addition to foliage, consider berries, such as cotoneaster and pyracantha, and seed pods, such as silver dollar and ornamental grasses. Interestingly shaped

▲ Restrained color
These tulips, narcissi, hostas, pansies, and viburnum provide a cool theme for an indoor display.

◄ Fragrant feast
Mixed lilacs and single white roses are the makings of a delightfully simple flower arrangement.

---

tip

When to pick
Cut flowers in the early morning or evening, when they are most turgid; flowers picked in midday heat are likely to wilt very quickly. Place newly cut stems immediately in a plastic bucket of water to prevent them from wilting.

► Rosy option
If space allows, grow a mixed collection of old-fashioned roses for picking and for garden scent.

winter branches, such as Pekin, or corkscrew willow (*Salix matsudana* "Tortuosa"), are brilliant for bulking out a single bloom or small bunch and creating a contemporary or oriental effect.

Plants for preserving Grow everlastings, or immortelles, for drying, such as strawflowers, annual sea lavender, statice, and achillea. Acanthus and thistles, such as globe thistles and sea holly, also dry naturally. Preserve foliage, such as beech, birch, and sweet chestnut, and flowers, such as bells of Ireland, in a mixture of half glycerine, half water, for supple material in rich autumnal tones.

Popular plants

These are just a few of the many plants useful in flower arranging.

Bells of Ireland (*Molucella laevis*): half-hardy annual with spikes of tiny white flowers, each surrounded by a green, shell-like calyx; prefers cool summers.

Delphinium (*Delphinium* spp., vars., and hybrids): hardy perennial, has spikes of blue, purple, mauve, or white flowers.

Elaeagnus (*Elaeagnus* spp., vars., and hybrids): quick-growing, hardy evergreen

Frothy green lady's mantle and velvety lamb's ears mix well, both outdoors and also in a cut display. They provide a good contrast to more vividly colored flowers.

▲ **Golden glow**
Elaeagnus x ebbingei "Gilt Edge" thrives in both sun and shade and provides year-round foliage that is perfect for cutting.

◄ **Bells of Ireland**
This unusual annual's elegant spikes of green, flower-like bracts can be preserved with glycerine.

tip

Pruning as you pick
When cutting shrub branches, cut back cleanly to just above a node, or growth point, and try to leave a well-balanced plant behind, so that it can go on to produce new, healthy growth.

shrub with glossy, gray-green, green, or variegated white-green leaves; small, fragrant flowers.

Hosta (*Hosta* spp., vars., and hybrids): herbaceous perennial has oval, heart- or lance-shaped leaves, often variegated; small, mauve, or white lily-like flowers.

Iris (*Iris* spp., vars., and hybrids): herbaceous and evergreen perennials and bulbs with generally sword-shaped leaves and flowers with three outer petals, or falls, three inner petals, or standards, and three strap-shaped petals, in a wide range of colors.

Lady's mantle (*Alchemilla mollis*): herbaceous perennial with lobed, light green leaves; sprays of tiny, starry, yellow-green flowers, which appear in the summer months.

Lilac (*Syringa* spp. and vars.): hardy, tree-like shrub with medium green leaves; pyramid-shaped panicles of purple, mauve, pink, or white, mostly fragrant flowers which can be seen from early to late spring, depending on species.

Lily (*Lilium* spp., vars., and hybrids): hardy bulbs with trumpet-shaped, often fragrant flowers; all colors but true blue, carried singly or in clusters.

Peony (*Paeonia* spp., and vars.): herbaceous perennials with globe- or bowl-shaped, single, semi-double or double

blooms in white, pink, rose, and crimson.

Pittosporum (*Pittosporum* spp. and vars.): moderately hardy evergreen shrubs with wavy-margined leaves, variegated in some forms.

Rose (*Rosa* spp., vars., and hybrids): hardy herbaceous shrubs and climbers. Unless you have the space to cultivate a selection, grow long-flowering hybrid

teas, floribundas, or the new English roses (named Austin, after the original breeder), which combine the long-flowering habit of modern roses with the luxurious beauty and scent of garden roses.

Tulip (*Tulip* spp., vars., and hybrids): hardy bulbs with cup- or goblet-shaped flowers in all colors but blue. Choose taller species for cutting.

ARRANGING SPRING BLOOMS

Generosity is the keynote for cut-flower displays in late spring, as growth gets well under way in the garden. At this time of year lilacs are at their best, and their opulent, fragrant blooms can provide the color and scale for impressive floral arrangements.

Rhododendrons flower in spring, too, and although they are not often used for cutting, rhododendrons do make ideal, large-scale floral infill.

Their mauve, pink, crimson, and white palette harmonizes perfectly with lilacs, and their dense, globe-shaped heads contrast well with lilac's pointed spikes.

Foliage is also essential in large displays, creating a restful green setting for the flowers, and a natural, uncontrived look. Lilac foliage is dull and deprives the flowers of water, so is normally removed during preparation, as is somber, unwieldy rhododendron

foliage. Substituting more attractive leaves is the best solution to the problem of providing greenery. Try eucalyptus, viburnum, and hosta, which make worthy partners for beautiful blooms.

▼ Pretty pastels
Dill, white lilacs, pink broom, and pink tulips are combined in an apple-green pitcher, for an informal, old-fashioned arrangement.

Choosing the material

It is possible to buy all the materials to make this arrangement, but the florist will need plenty of notice and it may be expensive. A better idea if you have a garden, is to create a similar display from your own resources.

Flowers An ordinary lilac, a deep red-purple variety, and pale pink rho-dodendron are shown, but you could use any forms of either, instead. Pink lilies, gladioli, Brompton stock, and sweet peas in shades of pink and mauve, repeat the theme; but white, richer pink, or purple sweet peas would be fine. Try to include a good proportion of pale material to lift the display.

If you are on a budget, substitute white spray carnations for the guelder rose, and omit the Brompton stock.

Foliage Eucalyptus and guelder rose foliage form the mainstay, with hosta leaves as accents, but most garden foliage will do, even golden privet or evergreen eunymous. Trailing or arching foliage, such as ivy, honeysuckle, or periwinkle, is especially valuable for creating a sense of movement in the arrangement and breaking the hard line of the container rim.

Making the arrangement

This front-facing display is based loosely on a symmetrical triangle, but the meandering outline, lack of focal point and generous, dense central infill counteract any hint of formality.

A simple, old-fashioned wooden hatbox is used for this arrangement, with a small waterproof bucket to hold the flowers. You could use a wine cooler or soup tureen as your outer container. Simple oriental garden tubs are also suitable, but always protect any polished furniture surface and remember to line any outer container.

▼ *Spring splendor*
Flowers in tones of pink, mauve, and white, set in a mass of greenery, create an elegant display.

Materials

Large container
Inner container, if necessary
Bricks or **upturned bowl**, if necessary
2in (5cm) mesh wire netting, 3 times the width of the container
wire and **bleach**
3 stems of pink lilies
2 rhododendron flower heads
15–18 lilac stems
6–8 *Viburnum opulus* (guelder rose) stems
2 large bunches sweet peas
1 bunch pale pink gladioli
4 stems eucalyptus foliage
1 bunch mixed Brompton stock
1 hosta leaf

MAKING THE DISPLAY

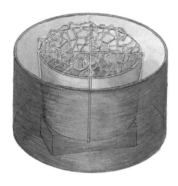

1 Preparing the foundation Place a bucket in the outer container. Rest it on a brick, so that its rim is just under the outer container's rim. Crumple netting to form a rough ball. Wedge it in the bucket, to mound partly above the rim. Thread wire through, and tie below. Fill bucket with water and a little bleach.

2 Setting the height and width Strip any leaves from the lilac. Place a lilac and lily stem centrally and well back, to set the height of the display, approximately twice the container's height. Place a slightly shorter lily stem to one side and a eucalyptus stem opposite. Using eucalyptus and lilac, set the width at twice that of the container.

3 Beginning the infill Strip the lowest leaves from the guelder rose branches. Insert two, roughly opposite each other near the base, to fill out the lower triangular shape. Insert one centrally, to hang over the front rim of the container and one, asymmetrically, near the top.

4 Adding lilacs and lilies Add the remaining lilac and lily stems. Vary the heights and try to make the stems look like they spring from the same central point. Continue to angle the lower stems downward.

5 Outlining the arrangement Insert the gladioli and Brompton stock, to add spikiness to the outline. Take care at this stage to avoid displacing any of the other flowers.

6 Build up the center Insert the two rhododendron flower heads and hosta leaf, low down and diagonally to one side, to avoid making the arrangement symmetrical. Use the sweet peas to create a star effect near the base, with a few, longer-stemmed outlying flowers. Stand back to check for gaps and adjust.

---

tip

Slitting stems
Cut a woody stem, such as a lilac or rose, at a 45° angle and then slit up the lowest 1in (2.5cm) of the stem using a craft knife or pair of scissors. This helps to improve the stems' intake of water. An alternative, more old-fashioned method, is to hammer the stem, as shown here.

Conditioning flowers

Sometimes it's a good idea to treat your cut flowers before you place them in the vase. Special treatments like those shown here often help to prolong the life of the cut flowers.

◀ Singeing stems

Some flowers, such as euphorbia, contain a white, milky sap which bleeds whenever the stem is cut. To seal the stem once it has been cut, hold the cut surface over a flame for a few seconds. Then give the flowers a long drink of water. This trick will also work for hellebores.

▼ Wiring stems

Internal wiring is a useful aid for hyacinths, tulips, and the like. Gently thread a florist's wire through the hollow stem and into the flower head. It is best to use a thin stick rather than wire to support amaryllis and hollyhocks, which are more delicate flowers and need careful handling.

▲ Pricking stems

Tulip stems can be pricked with a fine darning needle, just below the flower head. This will help to keep the stem straight and stop the tulip from drooping once it has been arranged.

▶ Boiling stems

Protecting the flowers in a cloth or tissue paper, place the cut ends of woody stems, such as those of roses, in 1in (2.5cm) boiling water for 1 minute. Follow with a cool drink.

FLOWERS FOR SUMMER DISPLAYS

The best time to create extravagant flower arrangements is summer. During this season the enormous range of flowers and foliage available from gardens and florists enables you to mix and match blooms, to make generous displays which would be out of the question at any other time of the year.

Many old-fashioned garden favorites, such as sweet peas, are grown commercially, so you can create a fresh-from-the-garden display even if you don't have a garden. Other good sources of flowers are bazaars and country fairs which provide a great excuse for a weekend outing as well as offering you the chance to pick up more unusual and inexpensive foliage.

You can base the color scheme of your display on mixed pastels, or, if you prefer, use a bolder mix of flowers. Alternatively, use a single color theme

▲ Summer medley
Philadelphus, larkspur, lady's mantle, and old-fashioned and species roses are all combined with Cornus variegata *in this side-table display.*

such as white or even tints of pink and red. A more sophisticated option is an all-green display with green flowers, seed heads, and foliage all in subtly different hues.

Inspirational material

Flowers Certain blooms such as old-fashioned roses, peonies, delphiniums, and campanulas have an inherent quality of summer, which helps to set the tone for a display, especially if some of the other flowers included, such as tulips, are not seasonal. Other summer flowers include hydrangeas, red-hot poker, and dahlias, as well as the perpetual blooms of hybrid tea and floribunda roses. As a rule, any combination of flowers that work well growing in close proximity will look good in a cut-flower display.

A huge bowl of one type of flower or very similar bloom, such as mixed cultivars of old-fashioned roses, can be effective; conversely, so can a mix that draws visual strength from deliberately contrasting shapes, sizes, and textures.

Foliage Garden foliage is a great summer bonus. Even plants as modest as privet or periwinkle can provide the bulk and green backdrop that transform a few flowers into a lush display. Colorful foliage, such as variegated dogwood or purple sage, can add depth to an arrangement and act as a visual bridge between flowers and solid green foliage. Less exciting foliage, such as eucalyptus or smilax also look good if used informally and generously. Pruning from hedges can also prove useful, but if you need to buy foliage from florists, avoid dark, mournful evergreens, such as box and cypress.

MAKING THE ARRANGEMENT

This front-facing display is loosely based on a low triangle. It features a mixture of summer flowers and foliage, building up to a dense center. If you use florist's roses, try to choose forms with flatter blooms that will open reliably and are long lasting; ask your florist if you are unsure. Traditional long-stemmed rose buds often wilt before they open. In a pinch, you can gently force long-stemmed rose buds open by placing the stems in warm water in a steamy room.

Silver foliage adds a special lightness, but is rarely available commercially. As an alternative, you could ask your florist to order white-variegated ivy, narrow-leaved eucalyptus, or bear grass.

The slightly raised bowl used in this display creates enough height for the material to arch gracefully. To get a similar effect, you can place a flat bowl on an up-turned saucer or shallow dish, but make sure they are stable. If in doubt, secure them with florist's adhesive before starting to arrange the flowers.

Materials

Bowl, florist's foam, prong, and **adhesive**
5–6 stems of *Artemisia ludoviciana*
l bunch **pink sweet peas**
2–4 branches of **flowering honeysuckle**
9–12 veronica flowers
7–8 marjoram flowers
8 deep pink roses
6 pale pink roses
5 stems **alchemilla**
2 stems **silver-leaf cineraria**
3–4 stems **baby's breath**
2 stems **flowering jasmine**
l bunch **lavender**

1 Start the display Place florist's adhesive in a cross shape in the base of the bowl. Press a prong firmly in the middle of it. Then impale foam, cut to fit the bowl snugly, onto the prong. The foam should project 1–2in (2.5–5cm) above the rim of the bowl.

2 **Setting the framework** Place a tall artemisia stem in the center and well back, to set the height. Use two sweet pea stems and one large honeysuckle branch on the right, and three veronica stems on the left, to set the width. Insert four artemisia, three marjoram, and five veronica stems as intermediate markers. Bring some forward, angled down, to break the rim line.

3 **Beginning infill** Cut the eight deep pink roses to varying lengths and form them into a sinuous "S" shape down the center. Place two pale pink roses at a low angle to one side, and four pale pink roses to the other side to give the arrangement depth. Insert the remaining sweet peas angled outward and downward to form three prongs, with a tight central cluster.

4 **Building up density** Add the remaining marjoram, honeysuckle, and veronica stems to increase density, especially towards the middle. Add five alchemilla stems, for color and textural contrast. Place two sprigs of silver-leaf cineraria on either side of the center, to frame the roses informally.

◀ *Scented splendor*
Old-fashioned roses and sweet peas form the central theme of this wonderful summer arrangement. The sprigs of lavender, jasmine, and honeysuckle all add extra fragrance to the display. If you want the floral arrangement to fit in with your interior, you could use roses of a different color.

5 **Finishing** Use sprigs of baby's breath to create a lacy contrast and fill any gaps. Insert sprigs of jasmine, some long, some short, to overhang the rim, and a bunch of lavender slightly off-center. As you proceed, check the display from the sides as well as the front, to ensure an even build-up.

tip

Fragrant delights
If you choose your flowers carefully, you can bring those wonderful summer scents indoors.

Stunning extras

You needn't confine yourself to the garden or florist for your raw material. The fresh vegetable department of your local supermarket can provide curled, crisp, and red-leaf lettuces, for use as cut foliage in flower arrangements.

In your own garden, dig up any lettuces that have gone to seed, roots and all, and wash the soil away. You'll be surprised how long-lasting they are when used in a floral display.

From the herb garden, pick large sprigs of parsley, dill, or fennel for adding a delicate touch. Purple sage and yellow variegated sage are also attractive in floral displays.

Fresh nasturtium flowers can be used in salads, so you may be able to obtain them at a delicatessen. You could float them in a shallow bowl of water, for a special table centerpiece.

▶ **Cool, calm, and collected**
Goldenrod, calla lilies, green flowers of Viburnum opulus, *and pink* Alstroemeria *repeat the color theme of the vase.*

▼ **Fun with foliage**
A dish of blue rue and red lettuce accompanies a typical summery mixture of pale yellow roses, acid-green euphorbia bracts, and rue, purple sage, and periwinkle foliage.

AUTUMN ARRANGEMENT

Fall, with its rich golden and red colors and harvest imagery, is a splendid season for making your own indoor flower arrangements, and even without flowers you can still create really impressive displays, such as the one shown here.

Pot et fleur, French for pot and flower, is the technique of combining cut material, whether flowers or, as here, leaves and berries, with any favorite houseplant in a stunning but temporary display. The plants provide a permanent supply of green or more colorful filler material, and cut flowers or branches of foliage vary the effect.

It's an economical way of creating impressive arrangements, since you can re-use the houseplants again and again, and a few cut flowers or branches of foliage go a long way.

The more houseplants you have, the wider your range of *pot et fleur*, so try to build up a collection of different houseplants, especially as some grow quickly, providing even more mass, virtually for free.

Foliage, flowers, and pot plants

Foliage In addition to the oak leaves shown, other colorful autumn foliage includes amelanchier, beech, hazel, birch, maple, flowering dogwood (*Cornus florida*), and many deciduous azaleas. Once leaves turn color, however, they can no longer take up water, so expect to replace them with fresh branches every few days.

Another solution would be to use glycerined foliage, which has autumnal tones and a supple texture, but is already fully preserved. Glycerined foliage branches should not need replacing.

Flowers Cotoneaster in berry is shown, but firethorn, barberry, snowberry, *Mahonia aquifolium,* or Oregon holly grape, hawthorn, and even rose hips are equally suitable, with berries ranging from white to yellow, orange, pink, scarlet, purple, and blue-black. For a dramatic effect, use leafless branches of crab apple.

If you want to include cut flowers with autumnal overtones, chrysanthemums, asters, sneezeweed, Guernsey lilies, African lilies, dahlias, and gladioli are all ideal.

Plants Virtually any houseplant with a small rootball can be used in a *pot et fleur*, from the trailing pothos to colored-leaved begonias and crotons,

ferns, bromeliads, ivy, or coleus potted up from the garden. Seasonal houseplants, such as pot "mums" or cyclamen, combine the natural attraction of flowers with longevity, providing weeks of color.

Whatever plants you choose, remember to water and feed them (if necessary) while they're hidden in the display.

It's also a good idea to rotate the plants you use in a *pot et fleur*, so they can recuperate in the temperature and light conditions that suit them best between their "tours of duty."

▲ A vibrant display
The focal point of this mixed foliage houseplant arrangement is a blushing bromeliad. Different pot plants will provide alternative color themes, so you can easily alter the emphasis to blend with your decor.

MAKING THE ARRANGEMENT

This front-facing display features oak and cotoneaster cut from the garden, and five small houseplants. If you have no garden, your florist can get glycerined beech or oak, and cotoneaster may be available. Wild blackberry or elderberry stems are another option.

Try to use branches that grow in flat sprays, rather than bushy ones. In a pinch, you can introduce the berry theme with berried houseplants such as winter cherry.

An eight-sided, oriental vase is used, but any wide-necked, waterproof container deep enough to hold the rootballs is fine. Stoneware, lined wicker baskets, or even enameled cookware would enhance the theme.

Materials

A wide oriental-style bowl or any vase of your choice
Florist's foam and **peat**
5 branches of oak, 4 cotoneaster branches
Small potted plants: 1 medium miniature palm, 1 medium weeping fig, 2 variegated dracaena plants (1 white, 1 pink), **1 medium blushing bromeliad** and **sphagnum moss**

1 Start the display If necessary, raise the levels inside the container with damp peat or sections of saturated florist's foam block, roughly cut to fit, so the surface of the rootballs come 1in (2.5cm) below the rim of the container. Some pots may be deeper than others.

2 Adding the plants Place the plants, still in their pots, in the container. Place the palm in the center, the weeping fig behind, the variegated dracaenas to the left and right, and, finally, the blushing bromeliad in front. Raise and tilt the bromeliad, so it faces toward the front and overhangs the rim, forming the focal point.

3 Adding the florist's foam To keep the plants in place and support the branches, tightly pack the space between the pots of the pot plants and the sides of the container with slabs of saturated florist's foam, roughly cut to fit. The larger the pieces of florist's foam, the more stable the overall effect will be.

4 Start framing the plants Remove the lowest leaves from 5 oak branches, and insert them in the florist's foam around the rim, to frame the plants. Use the tallest branches at the back and shorter ones in the front, to help conceal the pots and foundation.

5 Finishing Remove the lowest leaves and berries from 4 cotoneaster branches, and insert them here and there in the florist's foam, filling in spaces between the oak branches. For a neat, professional-looking finish, cover the surface with sphagnum moss.

A WINTER ARRANGEMENT

With their charming, old-fashioned appeal, informal dried-flower displays add a splash of color to a room. Dried flowers, seed heads, foliage, and grasses come in a huge range of natural and dyed tones and remain attractive for months on end. They are sold all year round, but are traditionally used during the winter, when fresh flowers are in short supply.

This particular display is based on rich autumnal tones, with no formal structure or focal point. For impact, it depends on a tapestry-like effect, with short-stemmed blooms hiding the stems of the taller flowers behind. On a tight budget, make a scaled-down version rather than a large, but sparse one. Try mixing contrasting forms like the typical intricate shape of roses, the solid globes of safflower or love-in-a-mist, the poker-like spikes of love-lies-bleeding, and the graceful, arching sprays of oats.

Most flowers are best grouped in small bunches, which makes building up a dense display quicker and easier than inserting individual stems. Use the dried rose and safflower leaves to add bulk and contrast.

Any opaque container is suitable,

▲ Winter warmer
This informal arrangement uses rich autumnal colors—reds, oranges, greens, and golds—which will add a touch of warmth to your home throughout the winter months.

but the rectangular terracotta garden pot shown, with its fruit and foliage swags, emphasizes the country theme. An oval wicker basket would be just as charming, and you could add a designer touch by lightly spraying it with aerosol spray paint to harmonize with the flowers.

Materials

Green love-lies-bleeding (*Amaranthus*)
1 bunch
Red love-lies-bleeding (*Amaranthus*)
1 bunch
Safflower (*Carthamus*) 1 bunch
Love-in-a-mist seed pods (*Nigella*)
1 bunch
Hydrangea flower heads 2–3
Crimson-dyed glixia 1 bunch
Red roses 2 bunches
Oats 1 bunch
1 rectangular or **oval container**
1 florist's dried flower foam block
1 florist's prong
Florist's adhesive
Medium-sized florist's wires

ARRANGING THE DISPLAY

1 Defining the shape Place florist's adhesive into the base, and press a prong onto it. Cut a foam block to fit, and impale it onto the prong. Using small bunches and single stems of love-lies-bleeding, define the display's height and width: 1½ times the container's height and slightly wider than the rim.

2 Filling in Cut the safflower and love-in-a-mist stems 1–2in (2.5–5cm) shorter than the love-lies-bleeding, and group into single-type clusters, stripping the lowest safflower leaves. Insert the clusters at random to begin building up a dome shape.

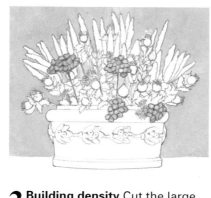

3 Building density Cut the large hydrangea flower heads into four sections. Loop a florist's wire through each section to form a stem, and insert at random, at the same height as the safflower. View from different angles as you work to make sure you have an even effect.

4 Adding red Group the glixia into bunches, since these are too small to be used singly. Cut the stems as for the safflower and insert at random. Cut the rose stems to come half way between the general mass and love-lies-bleeding, and remove the lowest leaves. Insert singly, in pairs and in small groups, filling in any large gaps as you do so.

5 Finishing Cut the oat stems at the same height as the roses and group into bunches. The oats are the palest and most eye-catching element, and need careful, even positioning. Stand back to check the arrangement, and reposition any oats that look out of place.

Oats

Love-in-a-mist

Hydrangea flower heads

Red roses

Crimson-dyed glixia

Green love-lies-bleeding

Safflower

Red love-lies-bleeding

DRIED FLOWER GARLAND

Wreaths and garlands are traditional wall and door decorations, usually associated with Christmas. But if you use dried flowers, bought at a florist's or dried at home, you can have garlands all year round.

Dried-flower garlands make delightful informal displays, perfectly at home in country-style settings. They can be used to brighten a dark corner and to decorate mirrors, mantelpieces and dressers. Hung on ribbons in harmonizing or matching colors, wreaths can make attractive substitutes for pictures in living rooms and bedrooms, whether placed alone or in groups of small garlands in complementary colors. A garland makes an excellent focal point for a dinner table, especially if you

choose colors to complement the food or your china. Finally, if your front door is sheltered in a porch, hang a dried-flower garland on it as a symbol of peace and friendship.

Although it can evoke the glories of summer gardens in full bloom, a dried-flower garland should never be treated like some poor relation of its fresh equivalent. Dried flowers have their own particular charms, notably the delicate, crisp textures and warm, muted colors. Unless you go for dyed ones, the subtle colors of dried flowers always complement one another, so your garland's color scheme can easily be designed to fit your existing decor or whatever preserved plant material is available.

▲ Perfectly preserved
The combination of dried flowers, seeds, and ears of wheat gives this garland a real country feel. Most of these flowers have kept their natural colors, but to add a touch of brightness, yarrow has been dyed a deep russet and used sparingly.

For a strong, assertive effect, try a combination of yellows, golds, and purples, or glowing reds and russets. A combination of palest yellows, golds, and silvers can suggest spring; yellows, oranges, and russets will suggest autumn. A Christmas wreath made from lichens, fir-cones, and white flowers would make a lovely wintry alternative to the traditional bright reds and glossy greens of holly and ivy.

A summery garland all year round
Using only dried flowers and foliage readily obtainable from florists, you can make an attractive country garland to adorn your house. It would look equally decorative in the hall, kitchen, bedroom, or living room.

Materials
Globe thistles, yarrow, strawflowers, wheat, silver dollar, poppy heads, delphiniums, sea lavender, helichrysum and Chinese puzzle are the ingredients of the garland.

Apart from the flowers, you will also need a medium-size **wire wreath frame**, a bag of **sphagnum moss**, **scissors**, a **craft knife**, **spool wire**, medium-gauge **florist's wire** bent into hairpin shapes, and a spool of **wreath wrap**.

MAKING THE GARLAND

1 Preparing the base Break up the moss and remove any twigs and dead matter. Attach one end of the spool wire to the frame. Tightly bind clumps of moss to the frame with spool wire until the whole ring is covered with a thick layer of moss.

2 Wrapping the garland Turn the garland over, and working from the back, bind the whole ring with wreath wrap. Overlap the tape slightly as you work, and secure each turn with a wire pin.

3 Covering with foliage Wire the wheat or other grassy foliage into clumps, then bind the clumps onto the frame with spool wire. Continue until the frame is covered with a thick layer of foliage.

4 Wiring bunches Holding the stem ends together and starting 2in (5cm) up, bend a piece of florist's wire behind the stems. Wind the long end of the wire around the stems down to the bottom of the bunch, and leave the ends extended to insert into the frame.

silver dollar

wheat

wreath frame and moss

scissors and craft knife

delphiniums

globe thistles

florist's wires

spool wire

strawflowers

helichrysum

Chinese puzzle

yarrow

poppy heads

sea lavender

wreath wrap

5 **Adding the flowers** To make sure the color in the arrangement is well balanced, start by inserting small bunches of flowers, wired individually, around the garland. Wire the flowers close to their heads or they will droop or snap off. Keep moving the garland around to view it from different angles.

6 **Completing the garland** Finish off by tucking in the silver dollar, Chinese puzzle and statice. The sea lavender can be wired together in small clumps. Aim for a wild and slightly unruly effect.

Infinite possibilities

Garlands are extremely versatile; they can be frivolous, festive, or formal, as the occasion demands. Working on bases of wire, vine, larch, or straw, you can use fresh or dried flowers and foliage, adding fruits or gourds or pinecones for extra interest and texture.

▼ Dye bright
You could transform a dark corner or gloomy hall with this vibrant garland. The contrasting colors of the flowers and foliage complement and intensify each other. Among the ingredients of the wreath are statice, mimosa, strawflowers, grasses, nigella, yarrow, and monkshood.

▲ From garden and the hedgerow
A rustic wreath that owes little if anything to the florist's art and proves that you can successfully dry all sorts of garden and field plants. The wire base is covered with hedgerow grasses and leaves, and then the dried flowers are dotted about, their muted colors blending easily.

◄ Seasonal color
The charm of a fresh wreath of glossy evergreen leaves can be enhanced as the season allows with fresh or dried Chinese lanterns, or, for Christmas, with berries and pinecones.

---

tip

Dry cleaning
If your garland becomes dusty over the months, use your hairdryer, set at a low heat, to gently blow the dirt away.

INDEX

PICTURE ACKNOWLEDGEMENTS

Photographs:
9 Garden Picture Library/Henk Dijkman; 10(t) Photos Horticultural, (b) Harry Smith Collection; 11(t) Philippe Ferret, (b) Harry Smith Collection, 12(t) Photos Horticultural, 13 Robert Harding Picture Library, 14 Eric Crichton, 15(t) Perdereau/Thomas, (b) Insight London Picture Library/Linda Burgess; 16(tl) Perdereau/Thomas, (tr) Elizabeth Whiting & Associates/Jerry Harpur, (b) Eric Crichton, 17 Photos Horticultural, 18(l) Garden Picture Library/Roger Hyam, (r) Garden Picture Library/Brian Carter, 19 Perdereau/Thomas, 20(t) Garden Picture Library/John Glover, (b) Eric Crichton, 21 Elizabeth Whiting & Associates/Ann Kelly, 22-3 Elizabeth Whiting & Associates/Ann Kelly, 24(t) Elizabeth Whiting & Associates/Ann Kelly, (bl) Houses and Interiors, 25 Elizabeth Whiting & Associates, 25 Eric Crichton, 26(t) Photos Horticultural, (b) Eric Crichton, 27 Lamontagne, 28(t) Eric Crichton, (b) S&O Mathews, 29 Eric Crichton, 30(t) Eric Crichton, (b) S&O Mathews, 31 Photos Horticultural, 32(t) Garden Picture Library/Jerry Pavia, (b) Photos Horticultural, 33 Garden Picture Library/Brigitte Thomas, 34(t) Photos Horticultural, (b) Garden Picture Library/Didier Willery, 36 Photos Horticultural, 37 Garden Picture Library/Ron Sutherland, 38 Garden Picture Library/Steven Wooster, 39(t) Lamontagne, (bl) Pictures Colour Library, (br) Lamontagne, 40(t) Garden Picture Library/Noel Kavanagh, (tr) Garden Picture Library/Vaughan Fleming, (b) Garden Picture Library/Henk Dijkman, 41(t) Garden Picture Library/Brian Carter, (b) Eaglemoss/John Suett, 42(t) Insight London Picture Library/Linda Burgess, (b) Eaglemoss/John Suett, 43(t) Lamontagne, (bl) Garden Picture Library/Brian Carter, (br) Eaglemoss/John Suett, 44(t) Edifice/Gillian Darley, (b) Lamontagne, 45 S&O Mathews, 46 Neil Holmes, 47(t) Photos Horticultural, (b) Marie-Louise Avery, 48(t,bl) Lamontagne, (br) S&O Mathews, 49 Eric Crichton, 50 Elizabeth Whiting & Associates/Karl-Dietrich Buhler, 51(t) Eric Crichton, (b) Photos

Horticultural, 52(tl) S&O Mathews, (tr) Garden Picture Library/Brian Carter, (b) Elizabeth Whiting & Associates/Anne Kelly, 53 Photos Horticultural, 54 Elizabeth Whiting & Associates/Jerry Harpur, 55 Garden Picture Library/Ron Sutherland, 56(t) Elizabeth Whiting & Associates/Karl-Dietrich Buhler, (b) Elizabeth Whiting & Associates/Jerry Harpur, 57(t) Eric Crichton, (b) Elizabeth Whiting & Associates/Marie OiHara, 58(t) Elizabeth Whiting & Associates/Karl-Dietrich Buhler, (b) Photos Horticultural, 59 Elizabeth Whiting & Associates/Jerry Harpur, 60(tl) Jon Bouchier, (c) Lamontagne, (b) Maison de Marie Claire/Kaluar, 61 Photos Horticultural, 62(t) Garden Picture Library/Ron Sutherland, (b) Neil Holmes, 63 Eric Crichton, 64(tl) Garden Picture Library/Ron Sutherland, (tr) Eric Crichton, (b) Neil Holmes, 65 Elizabeth Whiting & Associates/Jerry Harpur, 66 Jon Bouchier, 67(tl,bl)Insight London Picture Library/Linda Burgess, (cr) Jon Bouchier, 69 Insight London Picture Library/Linda Burgess, 70(t) Elizabeth Whiting & Associates/Jerry Harpur, (b) Andrew Lawson, 71(tr) Andrew Lawson, (bl) Garden Picture Library/Brian Carter, 72(t) Andrew Lawson, (c) Harry Smith Collection, (b) Jon Bouchier, 73 Elizabeth Whiting & Associates/Jerry Harpur, 74 Elizabeth Whiting & Associates/Spike Powell, 75(t) Elizabeth Whiting & Associates/Jerry Harpur, (b) Arcaid/Tim Soar, 76(t) The Stock Market, (b) The Conservatory Association, 77 Lamontagne, 78 Garden Picture Library/Brian Carter, 79 Biofotos/Heather Angel, 80(t) Garden Picture Library/John Glover, 80-81 Eric Crichton, 81(t) Sue Atkinson, 82(t) Garden Picture Library/Ron Sutherland, (tr,b) Eric Crichton, 83 Garden Picture Library/John Glover, 84 Lamontagne, 85(tl,b) Lamontagne, (tr) Photos Horticultural, 86 Photos Horticultural, 87 Garden Picture Library/Ann Kelly, 88(t) Eric Crichton, (b) Lamontagne, 89 Eric Crichton, 90(t) Lamontagne, (b) S&O Mathews, 91 Lamontagne, 92(t) Lamontagne, (c) Elizabeth Whiting & Associates/Karl-Dietrich Buhler, (b) Elizabeth Whiting

& Associates, 93(t) Lamontagne, (b) Elizabeth Whiting & Associates, 94(t) Elizabeth Whiting & Associates/Karl-Dietrich Buhler, (bl) Robert Harding Picture Library, (br) Eric Crichton, 95 Garden Picture Library/Marijke Heuff, 96 Insight London Picture Library/Linda Burgess, 97(t) Insight London Picture Library, (b) Garden Picture Library/Brian Carter, 98(t) Garden Picture Library/Brian Carter, (b) Insight London Picture Library/Linda Burgess, 99 Photos Horticultural, 100(b) Garden Picture Library/Brian Carter, 100-101(t) Robert Harding Picture Library, 101(b) Garden Picture Library/John Glover, 102(tl) Eric Crichton, (tr) Garden Picture Library/Brian Carter, (b) S&O Mathews, 103 Lamontagne, 104 Garden Picture Library/John Glover, 105(t) Photos Horticultural, (b) Eric Crichton, 106 Lamontagne, 107 Photos Horticultural, 108(t) Garden Picture Library/John Glover, (b) Elizabeth Whiting & Associates, 109(t) Garden Picture Library/John Glover, (b) Elizabeth Whiting & Associates/Jerry Harpur, 110(t) Garden Picture Library/David Russell, (b) Garden Picture Library/Brian Carter, 111 S&O Mathews, 112(t) Insight London Picture Library/Linda Burgess, (b) Lamontagne, 113(t) Garden Picture Library/Marijke Heuff, (b) Lamontagne, 114(t) Photos Horticultural, (b) Lamontagne.115 Lamontagne, 116(t) Lamontagne, (b) Elizabeth Whiting & Associates/Karl-Dietrich Buhler, (b) Elizabeth Whiting & Associates, 117(t) Lamontagne, (b) Elizabeth Whiting & Associates, 118(t) Elizabeth Whiting & Associates/Karl-Dietrich Buhler, 118(b) Robert Harding Picture Library, (br) Eric Crichton, 119 Lamontagne, 120(t) Lamontagne, (bl) Perdereau/Thomas, (br) Eric Crichton, 121 Eric Crichton, 122(t,cl) Eric Crichton, (b) Cent IdÉes/Maltaverne/Faver, 123 Photos Horticultural, 124-5 Lamontagne, 125(t) Photos Horticultural, 126(t) Lamontagne, (b) Eric Crichton, 127(t) Eric Crichton, (b) Garden Picture Library/Brian Carter, 128 Lamontagne, 129(t) Photos Horticultural, (b) Lamontagne, 130(t) Photos Horticultural, (b) Perdereau/Thomas, 131 S&O Mathews, 132(bl) Garden

Picture Library/David Russell, (br) Lamontagne, 133(t) Eric Crichton, (b) Lamontagne, 134(t) Eric Crichton, (b) Lamontagne, 135(t) Lamontagne, (r) Elizabeth Whiting & Associates/Jerry Harpur, 136(bl) Eric Crichton, 136-137(t) Lamontagne, 137(r) Elizabeth Whiting & Associates/Jerry Harpur, (b) Eric Crichton, 138(t) Eric Crichton, (bl) Insight London Picture Library/Linda Burgess, (br) S&O Mathews, 140 Photos Horticultural, 141(t) Photos Horticultural, (b) Eric Crichton, 142 Photos Horticultural, 143 Garden Picture Library/Clay Perry, 144(t) S&O Mathews, (b) Eric Crichton, 145(t) Garden Picture Library/John Glover, (b) Photos Horticultural, 146(t) Garden Picture Library/Clive Nichols, (b) Garden Picture Library/Brian Carter, 147 Eric Crichton, 148 S&O Mathews, 149(t,bl) S&O Mathews, (br) Photos Horticultural, 150(t) Eric Crichton, (b) Photos Horticultural, 151 Elizabeth Whiting & Associates/Di Lewis, 152 Robert Harding Picture Library, 153 Garden Picture Library/John Baker, 154(b) Garden Picture Library/Henk Dijkman, 154-5 S&O Mathews, 155(t) Garden Picture Library/Clive Nichols, (b) Garden Picture Library/Brigitte Thomas, 156(tl) Garden Picture Library/Brian Carter, (b) Photos Horticultural, (b) Eric Crichton, 157 Elizabeth Whiting & Associates/Di Lewis, 158-160 Merehurst Publications Ltd, 161 Elizabeth Whiting & Associates/Di Lewis, 162 Boys Syndication, 164(t) Elizabeth Whiting & Associates/Di Lewis, (b) Insight London Picture Library/Linda Burgess, 165 Garden Picture Library/Guy Bouchet, 167 Jon Bouchier, 168-171 Eaglemoss/John Suett, 172(tr) Robert Harding Picture Library, (cl) Elizabeth Whiting & Associates/Di Lewis, (b) Maison de Marie Claire/Marie-Paule PellÉ.

Illustrations:
68 Liz Pepperell/Garden Studios, 163 Michael Shoebridge, 166 Elisabeth Dowle, 168 Michael Shoebridge